VISUAL PRAYER:
How to Create a Spiritual Vision Board

By Dr. Crystal Green Brown

Foreword by Steve Fitzhugh

VISUAL PRAYER:
How to Create a Spiritual Vision Board

All content copyright 2015 & 2017 by Ask Dr. Cris, the Dream Life Doctor, LLC.

www.AskDrCris.com

All rights reserved. No part of this publication may be reproduced or redistributed in any form or by any mechanical or electronic means, including photocopying and recording, or by any information storage and retrieval system, without written permission of the publisher.

Published by The Dream Life Foundation

ISBN-13: 978-0692600924
ISBN-10: 0692600922

Printed in the United States of America Second Edition

1 **2** 3 4 5 6 7 8 9 10

Dedicated to the loving memory of
My Mother
Carolyn Jean Green

Special Thanks to:
God for guiding me to complete this book

Stevie Fitzhugh, thanks so much for your prayers, guidance, support and for writing the foreword for this book

Minister Michelle Wright of Second Calvary Baptist Church, thanks for providing your insight as the Scriptural Advisor

Sisters United of Second Calvary Baptist Church

Ken Davis for sharing your Habakkuk 2:2 story

Spiritual Vision Board Coaches: Alicia Domico, Lisa Alvarez, Susanne Calman & Cherisa Allen

Editor Meredith Nourie-Manuele

Leticia Parra & Desmond Stewart, Graphic Illustrators

Writers in the Spirit (WITS) Inspirational Writers Group under the leadership of Wayne Cooper

CONTENTS

Foreword: By Steve Fitzhugh	3
Chapter 1: What is the Difference Between a Vision Board and a Spiritual Vision Board?	12
Chapter 2: A Visual Form of Prayer	20
Chapter 3: Why Create and Use the Spiritual Vision Board?	32
Chapter 4: How Does the Spiritual Vision Board Work?	38
Chapter 5: How to Create a Spiritual Vision Board that Works!	48
Chapter 6: Ask	56
Chapter 7: Believe	80
Chapter 8: Receive	96
Chapter 9: Revise	104
Chapter 10: When is the Best Time to Create a Spiritual Vision Board?	112
Chapter 11: Spiritual Vision Board Examples	120
Postscript	168
References	172
About the Author	178

And the LORD answered me, and said, write the vision, and make it plain upon tablets, that he may run that reads it. For the vision is yet for an appointed time, but at the end it shall speak, and not lie: though it tarry, wait for it; because it will surely come, it will not tarry. Habakkuk 2:2-3

FOREWORD

After 30 years of engaging men, women and youth in the process of discovering their God-ordained life purpose, I have encountered very few people who have mastered the art of bringing hope to the heart like Dr. Crystal Green Brown (aka Dr. Cris). She gets it. *Visual Prayer* does in one book what takes some a lifetime to realize, that, no matter where you find yourself today, and no matter what condition life's turbulent vicissitudes have left you in emotionally, mentally or physically, there is always hope. And with the proper coaching, focused prayer and motivation, you can be the architect of a happier and more fulfilled you via your custom made spiritual vision board. Zig Ziglar, the great motivator, would frequently say, "The fundamental value of all change is hope. The engine upon which hope runs is called encouragement." Dr. Green Brown and the spiritual vision board coaches featured throughout this book facilitate the process by which we all can embark upon the life-long journey of self-improvement and become the best version of ourselves that we can possibly be, while in pursuit of life's highest good. This type of real change takes vision.

We all have, at some time, experienced those inexplicable plateaus in life where it seems our engines have stalled, and our future is undefined. Feeling stuck, we soon find ourselves proclaiming in exasperation, "There's got to be more to life than this!" You are not stuck, friend; this is not the end; it's just the process. The process prepares you for the promise. You can't control what happens to you, but you can certainly determine where you go from here. It's likely easy for us to look over our shoulders and recall that age in our lives when we bustled with a hope of who we'd like to become, what we'd like accomplish and what our world of family, friends and life would potentially look like one day. It was probably during a simpler time, before the cares, stresses and temptations of life dogged us, before adult failure disappointed us, before lost love scarred us. *Visual Prayer* depicts for us a graphic, welcomed, and daily reminder that, as long as we have breath, there is hope. Yes, prayer changes things. *Visual Prayer* warns us not to allow today's darkness to cause us to doubt the great promises God spoke in the light. Adversity comes to unseat us. Warfare will always contend with promise. What a tragedy to cave into our doubts and become reduced to an aimless wanderer, having sight but no vision simply because of the arrival of opposition.

    We may not remember when exactly it was that we stopped believing. We just know that we stopped. Maybe it was the path of least resistance that enticed you to abandon the struggle of getting back up after a fall? Was it fear, that great paralyzer of progress, that has kept you from risking the vulnerability to love again, wish again, reminding you of the rawness of your pain? Truth is, there is no suffering that we endure today that's even worthy of being compared to the joy that will be revealed in us tomorrow. Spiritual vision boards help by showing us that the *first* report is not the *last* report. On the contrary, true champions do not succumb to the forces of evil; instead, we battle with weapons that are not carnal or common but mighty enough to pull down strongholds and demolish arguments that rise up against us. We use our hearts to dream the vision, then our minds to document and display, knowing with certainty that greater is He that is in us, inspiring vision, than He that is in the world, discouraging vison. In this book, we clearly come to understand the value of using our positive imagination to courageously take off our coats, make dust in the world and build our boards! When we do, we will witness the remarkable and testify to the impossible as we gain personal strength and vigor throughout the journey. Typically, our conservative cautious requests are no challenge to God's genius. He is abundantly capable. So don't relent. Jump in with gusto! Arise and build. It has been my experience that God gives us ideas bigger than ourselves so that by the stretching of our faith, we afford Him the joy of pulling the impossible within our reach. Our spiritual vision boards should test the limits, place a demand on the resources of heaven and be bigger than ourselves. Through our spiritual vision board, we have permission to dream the ridiculous and imagine the impossible.

The release of *Visual Prayer* not only puts testimony on display, but it is also relevant and timely. Isn't that just like God? Biblical truths tend to always speak to us in season. New research is finally catching up with the Bible. Today, scientists can prove that fruit from our spiritual vision boards, i.e., focused healthy thinking, sustained targeted prayer, encouragement and hope, all yield measurable changes in our emotional and physical selves, even our DNA. Dr. Caroline Leaf, in her groundbreaking work *Switch On Your Brain,* asserts that because of today's technological advances in science and research, we can now scientifically validate what the faith community already knows and believes: the tenets of God's Word pertaining to—but not limited to—our emotional, mental and physical health are true. What we commit our minds to think about is directly proportional to our mental, emotional and physical well-being. Whatever is true, whatever is noble, whatever is right, whatever is pure, whatever is lovely, whatever is admirable, if anything is excellent or praiseworthy, think about such things (Philippians 4:8).

That is precisely what *Visual Prayer* challenges us to do every day. If thinking on these things brings value, should seeing a replica of them on our spiritual vision boards as we pray sustain that value? Emphatically YES! And the God of peace will be with you (Romans 4:9b). You will experience this peace in your mind, emotions and body.

A spiritual vision board is a simple, common sense idea that yields grand results. By default, it demands that we think forward, dream bigger, hope deeper and pray without ceasing. And in so doing, we will eliminate dis-ease from our lives. This is an inclusive promise, regardless of who you are, where you are from, who you are from or what you look like. "We are not prisoners of our biology," Dr. Leaf explains. Genetic markers from our parents may *predispose* us to a certain inherited potential, but the evidence today shows those markers do not necessarily *predetermine* who we will become. We have the free will to choose and believe. And by our choices, we redefine our existence, bringing influence to four generations, be it positive and healthy or toxic and unhealthy. Isn't it time for your season? Isn't it time for you to believe for you?

My spiritual vision board is still working for me. It may not have been as articulate and defined, as Dr. Cris has now revealed in *Visual Prayer*, as it could have been or should have been, but it works. I am a man of prayer and faith. Vision is prominent in my life but not because it is a gimmick. There is a new gimmick every day; gimmicks come and go. A spiritual vision board bathed in prayer, inspired by God and buttressed by faith, becomes a lifestyle. Of the 10,000 college football players each year who dream of playing in the National Football League, only 3.3 percent will ever get to play one down. I was one, because of vision. How did a quiet kid like me from Akron, Ohio end up traveling all over the world as an international motivational speaker? Vision! How did a youth advocate like me broker the purchase of three former crack houses in Washington, DC's most underserved and notorious southeast communities and transform them into an after school teen drop-in center as a safe-haven for at-risk youth? Vision! How did that same champion for youth receive a $450,000 government grant for this faith-based youth center (although he was told they don't give government funds to faith-based nonprofits) to establish a state-of-the-art recording studio, computer lab and job placement academic center? Vision! When you follow hard after the vision, provision will hunt you down! A humble visionary, I learned that God does not call the qualified; He qualifies the ones that He calls. Today, I am still adding to my spiritual vision board. I was recently given 405 acres of pristine mountainside, surrounded by 12,000 acres of protected national forest, to steward into the best Christian camp and retreat facility 405 acres can accommodate. How will I do it? Visual Prayer! I have adopted Steven Spielberg's motto, "Dream for a living!"

After reading this book, you too will definitely be enlightened. But if after you have been enlightened, visual prayer does not begin, it will be as if you had never been exposed to this work. It will be as if your enlightenment never happened. This book is full of information for you to succeed with your custom-made spiritual vision board. In my work today as a certified NFL Transition Coach, I mentor NFL retirees as they attempt to live life successfully without their lifetime identity of football. One way I support them is by sharing information that will enlighten and equip. I tell them incessantly that information minus application equals information. Information plus application equals transformation. Maybe God will show you, through this book, how you, too, can end conformity and begin transformation with your spiritual vision board. As you commit to *Visual Prayer*, you will be amazed at what will come to mind that's already hidden in your DNA secretly yearning to be born on your spiritual vision board. Happy Visioning!

Steve Fitzhugh
President, Covenant Village Retreat
Certified NFL Transition Coach

Chapter 1: What?

What is the Difference between a Vision Board and a Spiritual Vision Board?

What is the Difference between a Vision Board and a Spiritual Vision Board?

"Write the vision, and make it plain"
Habakkuk 2:2

Our minds respond strongly to visual stimulation. A powerful way to bring our goals to fruition is by creating vision boards that use pictures, images, and affirmations as a tangible representation of our dreams, goals, and ideal life. Although vision boards have been around for years, recently they have grown in popularity. They (vision boards) have become so popular, that sometimes it may be easy for some of us to overlook their origin and perhaps give credit to others.

The Law of Attraction

Of all the books that I've read, webinars that I've seen, and meetings that I've attended, the only aspect of the vision board that most instructors speak of is the law of attraction. Not that anything is wrong with the law of attraction, but this is not one of those books. This book shares what few, if any, vision board book shares: primarily that biblical principles are the foundation of the vision board process. It is because of these biblical principles that I refer to vision boards as *spiritual* vision boards. Quite simply, the primary difference between traditional vision boards and spiritual vision boards is that the latter acknowledges biblical principles and God's promises, where the former acknowledges the law of attraction as its source of inspiration.

When I first started using the phrase spiritual vision boards on social media, a few people chimed in with their opinions on what they believed a spiritual vision board should be, and I appreciate their thoughts and opinions. However, I think that it is important for us to keep in mind that God gave us all free will to choose whatever we like and choose to acknowledge. But for me and my house, we choose to serve and acknowledge the Lord (Joshua 24:15).

For those of you who may desire a further explanation on the difference between vision boards and spiritual vision boards, please refer to the postscript in the back of this book. In that section, I discuss more about not only the difference between the two boards, but I also share my perspective on God's expectation for His children.

How This Book Will Help You

Specifically, this book is designed to assist followers and non-followers of Christ with the following:

1. Learn how God's promises and biblical principles are directly connected to the spiritual vision board process
2. Learn how to connect your goals, visions, and desires of heart with God's plans and purpose for your life
3. Understand how you can be a co-creator of your own destiny with God as your partner
4. Understand how the spiritual vision board process can be used as a visual form of prayer
5. Learn how to prepare for creating a spiritual vision board
6. Understand how to activate your spiritual vision board with faith, spiritual enlightenment, gratitude, visualization and giving
7. Learn how to take physical possession of your gifts and blessing
8. Understand how doubt and dead prayer can prevent you from receiving the desires of your heart
9. Learn of the most opportune times to develop your spiritual vision board

10. Finally, but most importantly, learn how developing a deeper and more profound relationship with our heavenly Father can change your life.

One of the coaches, who has been instrumental in helping with this book, shared with me her experience on how the (spiritual) vision board process has helped her to know and establish a personal relationship with Jesus. I believe that so many of you can make a similar connection.

I believe, that there are so many people in the world today who are searching for more out of life. Searching for a connection to something or someone that is bigger and grander than they could ever imagine. That missing component may or may not be the creation of a spiritual vision board, but I do believe that developing a deeper relationship with God and perhaps creating a tangible representation of your communication with Him may be helpful in filling a void left empty by our daily routines.

The spiritual vision board process can be viewed as an ongoing record of your prayer requests, communication and connection with God. Sometimes we may have asked God for something, and when it did not happen right away, we simply forgot about it. However, when using the spiritual vision board, you can revisit those moments of asking, and continue to be thankful for all the blessings that God has given you.

Therefore, I encourage you to read this book, share it with others and discover how you can change your life by simply developing your very own spiritual vision board.

God Bless.

Chapter 2: A Visual Form of Prayer

A VISUAL FORM OF PRAYER

A Visual Form of Prayer

"The Lord has heard my cry for mercy, the Lord accepts my prayer"

Psalm 6:9

A few years ago, I began conducting spiritual vision board workshops for a career group at St. John Episcopal Church in Charlotte, NC. It was at one of these workshops that a participant asked, "What is a (spiritual) vision board?" So I shared a brief explanation of my interpretation of the (spiritual) vision board process, noting the use of images, affirmations, and mantras on a physical board along with other details. Then

another participant chimed in and added, "Do you mean the (spiritual) vision board is a visual form of prayer?" A light bulb went off, and I agreed. "Yes, that's exactly what it is—a **visual form of prayer**."

Usually, when we request our desires of God, we do so verbally; simply asking for whatever it is that our hearts desire. But when we add another aspect to our prayer requests by making them visual instead of just verbal, we add another dimension to our prayer experience while making our requests clear and plain. When responding to Habakkuk's plea, God made this suggestion: "Write the vision, and make it plain upon tables, that he may run that readeth it" (Habakkuk 2:2). I'll share more about this scripture when we review biblical precepts in Chapter 5 on *How Does a Spiritual Vision Board Work?*

But what we should gather from God's instruction is to take on the full spectrum of our prayer experience. We should recognize that our prayer experience should not just be verbal and also visual, but, most importantly, clear and plain, as He suggested to Habakkuk. That is when we should show God what it is that we desire. Not only are we showing Him the depth and breadth of our requests with exact colors, shapes and sizes, but we are also confirming for ourselves the details in which we desire a particular aspect—details that mere words cannot always indicate, but visual images can clarify. Keep in mind He said, "…make it (your vision) plain."

Some may dispute the use of imagery in prayer, stating that God's request to Habakkuk was to write it down on tables in the King James version and on tablets in the New International version. Basically, not to draw it. However, when we consider exactly what a vision is, can we not agree that visions usually take on a pictorial form? Usually, these visions are bright and colorful. These vivid depictions can best be illustrated in picture form. I think that is probably why social media sites such as Pinterest and Instagram receive so much interest; because we are visual people who thrive on the beauty that can be captured and appreciated by images.

A great example of using scripture Habakkuk 2:2 to the fullest can be best illustrated by a fellow author and friend, Ken Davis. I had the pleasure of meeting Ken and his lovely wife, Pricilla, at a writer's meeting (WITS- Writers in the Spirit) that we are both members of. After conducting a spiritual vision board workshop for the writer's group perhaps a year or two ago, Ken chimed in to share his experience with using scripture Habakkuk 2:2. The following excerpt is Ken's story in his own words.

Ken Davis' Story

As a vocational coordinator at Fort Hope, a faith-based rehab ministry of PTL in Fort Mill, SC for men, I had the responsibility of developing vocational training programs for the men. One of the programs I was developing involved the completion of an auto shop. The plan was for this to be a lube shop and minor repair service center for partners, employees and the local public.

I was having a challenge in getting the attention of the construction crews at the ministry to come to the fort and complete the shop. They were all involved in various other building projects, and my shop was way down on their list of priorities. This became quite frustrating for me to say the least.

One afternoon, while sitting in my office, I asked the Lord what I needed to do to get things moving forward. That's when I found Habakkuk 2:2. As I read and meditated on this scripture, the thought came to me to write the vision for this unfinished shop as a brochure complete with the services available, time open and numbers to call for service.

Having completed the rough draft, I called a friend who had a printing company in Charlotte, NC and told him that I needed to have these brochures printed for the service shop. I took him the draft, and in three days, he called me with the brochures completed. I remember how excited I felt when I went to pick them up.

On my way back to Fort Hope with my brochures in hand, I asked the Lord what I should do next. I heard a voice in my spirit tell me to show a brochure to the first person I encountered when I entered the gate to the Fort. I got out of my car with brochure in hand, walked through the gate, and what happened next was so amazing.

The first person I encountered was Wayne Sassier, who just happened to be the head of all the construction crews at the ministry. When I showed him my brochure, he asked, "Can I use your phone?" Upon my reply, he ran to my office, called to another location on the grounds, and instructed one of the construction crews to stop what they were currently doing and come to the Fort. "Ken has a shop he needs to have finished, and we need to get on it," Wayne said. In three days, my shop was completed, and in two weeks, we were open for business!

Isn't that amazing? What occurred is exactly what Habakkuk 2:2 says. When I showed my vision to Wayne, which I had written down and had printed in the brochure, he literally ran to my office—as if he was straight out of Habakkuk 2:2—and got things moving toward completion of my vision. You can read more about this story in Ken's book titled *7 Keys to Successful House Groups*.

Vision of a New Car

This next story is a personal one that occurred during the late 1990s, before I started using spiritual vision boards. But the process that I went through confirmed how having a vision and using visual imagery as a form of prayer can be an aide to my prayer experience.

The last time I decided to purchase a new car, before the car that I'm driving now, it took perhaps a few months before I narrowed my vision down to the right make, model and color. I had already owed a Celica, but the body style of the models that were made during the middle to late 1990s are one of a kind, simply classic and elegant. So, I asked God to bless me with the latest version at that time, with a sunroof, spoiler, and either teal or periwinkle in color. I thought both colors were feminine, girly and cute. Then I called around to every Toyota dealership within a 50-mile radius and told them exactly what I was looking for. And I did one more thing because these cars were so rare and hard to find. I called a Toyota manufacturer and shared with them the difficult time that I was having securing the car of my dreams. Before I go on with my story, notice what I did to receive my blessing. I called various dealerships in the area and also contacted a Toyota manufacturer. In other words, I took an active role in the receipt of my blessing. I didn't just sit around waiting for my new Celica to fall out of the sky. I took part in what God was planning for me. You'll learn more about this part of the spiritual vision board process when reading *receiving* your blessing in Chapter 8.

I called a Toyota manufacturer and shared with them my desire, so they shipped a brand new Celica to a dealership that was about 7 miles from my house. I test drove it, kept it overnight and absolutely loved it. But there was one problem, the Celica was white and not teal or periwinkle. Although it was difficult to return the new Celica back to the dealership the next day, I knew that I was doing the right thing. However, driving this car solidified my desire to own it. While it was in my possession, I felt unspeakable joy. The smile on my face was so wide I could hardly contain myself, which leads me to another point: visualization is another step in the receipt of your blessing. In order to receive, we must first *believe*. I will review more on the visualization process in Chapter

7, which shares the principle of believing.

Several months later, a dealership in Canton, OH—which is about 25 minutes south of Akron—contacted me and said that they had my car. I asked the salesperson a few questions about the mileage, color and a few other details, and everything checked out. Even before seeing it, I knew God had blessed me with my gift. So, I placed a deposit on the car over the phone, sight unseen. Needless to say, I was not disappointed when I arrived at the dealership. Having done my homework, I made a fair offer and, once they had added a spoiler per my request, I drove home in my new teal Celica. That was close to 20 years ago.

I loved that car so much that I continued to drive it until I knew that God was ready to bless me with something bigger and better. So, I repeated the process for the most part by selecting a new vehicle (a powder blue Lexus), placing it on my board and test driving it. Instead of calling around to dealerships in the area, it was easier this time because I conducted an internet search. I narrowed my selection down to three vehicles that were identical in make, model and color, and although the entire process still took close to a year, I'm happy to say that God blessed me with my new powder blue Lexus right before Christmas of 2016, and I'm so thankful!

As mentioned in chapter 1, this book is different from any other vision board book that you will find because it specifically addresses the biblical principles associated with the spiritual vision board process and how you can use this process as part of your prayer life. Therefore, every time the words "vision board" are used, the word *spiritual* will precede it because of the biblical principles and promises associated with it. But please know that, whether you choose to use a spiritual vision board or not, God does answer prayer. And I know that so many of you believe in the power of prayer and include it as a part of your daily lifestyle. But have you ever experienced a prayer request that went unanswered, a prayer that you believed was your time or season to receive, but for whatever reason it didn't come to fruition? More often than not, this can be the norm for so many of us. Therefore, it helps to know **what, why, how and when** the spiritual vision board works. Additionally, I discuss more about unanswered prayer in Chapter 9 on *revising* your spiritual vision board. Specifically, I will share with you what God shared with me in the phrase *dead prayer*.

These next chapters will answer all of those questions and provide a better understanding of the practical yet spiritual nature of using spiritual vision boards.

Chapter 3: Why?

Why Create and Use a Spiritual Vision Board?

Why Create and Use a Spiritual Vision Board?

"For I know the plans I have for you"
Jeremiah 29:11

Now that you know what a spiritual vision board is, let's move on to why you should create and use one. Knowing that the spiritual vision board adds depth, breadth, and a clearer perspective to your prayer experience, we can also agree that by using the spiritual vision board, our communication with God takes on another dimension which includes adding a visual component to our existing verbal component. Some of us, if not most of us, can admit that our prayers, on occasion, seem to go unanswered. It's almost like our prayers are somehow lost in the shuffle of other prayer requests.

Prayer requests for better relationships, more money, or that dream job which could fulfill your purpose in life… Does any of this sound familiar? If you said yes to one or more, I'm not surprised. Because at almost every spiritual vision board workshop that I've instructed, these same prayers are what most people often request. I can share with you that since I've started using the spiritual vision board as a daily part of my prayer life, these requests have been answered. So, when you ask why should you create and use the spiritual vision board in the first place, one good reason can be how it solidifies your prayer experience. Using the spiritual vision board helps to clarify the desires of your heart and brings your desires to the forefront so that it's easier to focus on them. For example, what make, model, and color car would you like? If you're looking for Mr. Right or Mrs. Right, what would he or she look like? What characteristics would he or she possess? Or when looking for your dream job, what field would you prefer to work in? Do you have a preference in working on particular days of the week or hours of the day? When it comes to your dream job, what are your *must haves*? What will get you out of bed in the morning with excitement to start another work day? These are the questions that, with specific direction and clarity of purpose, your spiritual vision board can help you achieve.

God Loves All of Us

What we need to be mindful of is that "God is no respecter of persons" (Acts 10:38), which basically means God is not partial to any one person or another. It may appear that some people are simply lucky, that they live lives that are golden and everything they touch prospers; while on the surface, this may appear to be true, in reality, God loves all of His children. He desires that we enjoy life and live it to the fullest (John 10:10). And what better way is there than to use prayer to its fullest capability?

Plans We Make

Have you ever made a plan for your life that either did not include God, or you simply thought that it was O.K. to proceed without asking God first? In the next chapter, when we review how the spiritual vision board works, we will review the importance of keeping God first in everything that we think and do. This includes our plans for the future. So very often, we go about our day thinking about obtaining this or doing that, but how often do we stop and think how these plans align with God's will for us? In Proverbs, Solomon shares with us that "People make plans in their minds, but only the Lord can make them come true. Depend on the Lord in whatever you do, and your plans will succeed" (Proverbs 16:1, 3). Simply put, in everything we do and think about, include God in the process, and He will complete your vision because sometimes we don't know exactly what God may have in store for us; His plans are much larger and grander than we could ever imagine. Jeremiah 29: 11-13 tells us

> *For I know the plans I have for you, declares the* LORD, *plans*
> *to prosper you and not to harm you, plans to give you hope and a future.*
> *Then you will call on me and come and pray to me, and I will*
> *listen to you. You will seek me and find me when you seek me with*

all your heart.

How is it that some of us forgot to include this essential aspect in our prayer life – putting God first. In concluding this chapter on why to create and use the spiritual vision board, think of it as a testimony. Everyone should have a testimony and be able to share with others how God has blessed them. In the last chapter, I shared with you Ken's testimony on getting an auto shop built in just 3 days after he turned his vision into a brochure. My testimony was of a teal Celica that I was blessed with close to 20 years ago, and most recently taking that Celica to the next level with a powder blue Lexus. You, too, will have a testimony because you will receive results that you never experienced before by choosing to make your vision plain and by communicating with God more effectively.

Chapter 4: How?

How Does the Spiritual Vision Board Work?

How Does the Spiritual Vision Board Work?

*"Before all your people I will do **wonders** never before done in any nation in all the world. The people you live among will see how awesome is the work that I, the LORD, will do for you"*
Exodus 34:10

When we know the Bible, specifically God's principles, precepts, and promises, we should also know that these foundational aspects can aid in our personal relationship with God. And it is through that personal relationship that we can align our purpose with God's will which aids in our development of the spiritual vision board construction process. In Romans, we learn that we must be changed and transformed from within. And it is through this transformation process that we become aligned to His will for our lives. Romans 12:2 shares:

Do not change yourselves to be like the people of this world, but be changed within by a new way of thinking. Then you will be able to decide what God wants for you; you will know what is good and pleasing to him and what is perfect.

Let's review some of God's basic principles or precepts and how you can apply each to the development of your spiritual vision board.

Four Biblical Principles

1. Ask Believe and Receive

In Matthew 21:22, we learn that "And all things, whatsoever ye shall *ask* in prayer, believing, ye shall *receive*."

Where some may error is simply on the part of not asking or asking with the wrong motives. James 4:2-3 says, "You do not have because you do not ask God. When you ask, you do not receive, because you ask with wrong motives, that you may spend what you get on your pleasures." We cannot receive all that God has for us if we don't ask Him for His blessings; most importantly, we have to ask with a bigger purpose in mind. That purpose is to unite our will with His. The best way to do this is by putting Him first in all we do. Joyce Meyer says it best in her book, a daily devotional, *New Day New You*: "If you put God first in your finances, first in your time, first in your conversation, first in your thought, first in your decisions, your life will be a success."

2. Ask, Seek, Knock

Also in Matthew (7:7), we find the scripture, "Ask and it will be given to you; seek and you will find; knock and the door will be opened to you. For everyone who asks receives; the one who seeks finds; and to the one who knocks, the door will be opened. Similar to Matthew 21:22, we know that God responds to our verbal requests of Him. What we are willing to ask for, He is willing to provide. However, this scripture calls for more on our part than faith (believing). This scripture incorporates the importance of taking part in our blessings by being physically active (seeking and knocking). There is one more scripture that we need to be mindful of when it comes to seeking, in Jeremiah 29:13, God asks that we seek Him, "And ye shall seek me, and find me, when ye shall search for me with your heart."

3. Write the vision and make it plain

In Habakkuk 2:2, we learn that this prophet pleaded with God for direction and understanding. And God replied, "Write the vision, and make it plain upon tables, that he may run that readeth it."

When combining these first two principles, a simple 3-step process is revealed. It's this step-by-step process that I use as a model to assist others in developing their spiritual vision boards during my workshops. The steps are as follows:

Step 1) Write down your vision clearly and plainly - ASK

Step 2) Use faith to activate your requests - BELIEVE

Step 3) Be prepared to take action through seeking and knocking - RECEIVE

In our next chapter, "How to make the spiritual vision board," these simple, step-by-step instructions will provide you with the guidance you need to construct your own spiritual vision board. For now, let's go back to the final, but most important, biblical principle.

4. *Put God first*

In Proverbs 3:6 (TLB), King Solomon suggests that "In everything you do put God first." In Matthew 6:33 (ASV), we are asked to seek first His kingdom. Again, in Jeremiah 29:13, we are asked to seek Him and we would find Him when we search with all our heart. God said to Abraham, "Walk [habitually] before Me [with integrity, knowing that you are always in My Presence], and be blameless and complete" (Genesis 17:1 AMP). This last example comes from Psalm 37:4 "Delight thyself also in the Lord: and he shall give thee the desires of thine heart." So what does it mean to put God first?

Putting God first starts with a decision. This decision includes developing an intimate relationship with Him. God is more important than anything else, more important than our job, our family, climbing the corporate ladder, whatever and whomever. Our relationship with God sets the benchmark for who we are in Christ. By putting Him first, we have to make it a habit to pray constantly and consistently throughout the day, to stay in His Word, and spend time in His presence. Consider how you would treat a person that you admire and desire to spend the rest of your life with. That is how we must treat Him. Allow God to know that we love, honor, and respect Him so much that our lives are meaningless without Him. Remember what Joyce Meyer shared with us about putting Him first in everything that we do. This step is the most crucial step. **Start with God first.**

God's Promises & Blessings

We know that life is not always easy. Sometimes we may struggle daily with any number of disappointments, difficulties or dilemmas. But we also know that with God all things are possible (Matthew 19:26). "All things work together for good for those who are called according to His purpose" (Romans 8:28). And if we simply delight ourselves in Him, He will give us the desires of our heart (Psalm 37:4).

These scriptures are just a few of the basic promises that we can use as a source of strength and encouragement when times get tough. But we should also know that, beyond these general promises, God has also shared with us specific promises to bless any and all situations.

Promises of **comfort**: "God is the Father who is full of mercy and all *comfort*. He comforts us every time we have trouble, so when others have trouble, we can *comfort* them with the same *comfort* God gives us. We share in the many sufferings of Christ. In the same way, much *comfort* comes to us through Christ" (2 Corinthians 1:3-5).

Promises of **courage**: "*Don't be afraid* because I have saved you. I have called you by name, and you are mine. When you pass through the waters, I will be with you. When you cross rivers, you will not drown. When you walk through fire, you will not be burned, nor will the flames hurt you. This is because I, the Lord, am your God, the Holy One of Israel, your Savior" (Isaiah 43:1-3).

Promises of **faith**: "Now *faith is* the substance of things hoped for, the evidence of things not seen. For by it the elders obtained a good report. Through faith we understand that the worlds were framed by the word of God, so that things which are seen were not made of things which do appear. But without faith it is impossible to please Him, for He that cometh to God must believe that He is, and that He is a rewarder of them that diligently seek Him" (Hebrews 11: 1-6).

Promises of **guidance**: "The Lord will *always lead you*. He will satisfy your needs in dry lands and give strength to your bones. You will be like a garden that has much water, like a spring that never runs dry" (Isaiah 58:11).

Promises of **hope**: "The Lord's love never ends; his mercies never stop. They are new every morning; Lord, your loyalty is great. I say to myself, 'The Lord is mine, so I hope in Him.' The Lord is good to those who *hope* in Him; to those who seek Him" (Lamentations 3:22-25).

Promises of **love**: "We know the love that God has for us, and we trust that love. God is love. Those who live in love live in God, and God lives in them" (1 John 4:16).

Promises of **patience**: "My brothers and sisters, when you have many kinds of troubles, you should be full of joy, because you know that these troubles test your faith, and this will give you *patience*. Let your patience show itself perfectly in what you do. Then you will be perfect and complete and will have everything you need" (James 1:2-4).

Promises of **prosperity**: "Good will come to the man who trusts in the Lord. He will be like a tree planted by the water, that sends out its roots by the river. It will not be afraid when the heat comes but its leaves will be green. It will not be troubled in a dry year or stop giving fruit. (Jeremiah 17:7-8).

Promises of **strength**: "He gives *strength* to those who are tired and more power to those who are weak. The people who trust the Lord will become strong again. They will rise up as an eagle in the sky; they will run and not need rest; they will walk and not become tired" (Isaiah 40: 29, 31).

When we study His word, we learn that there are promises for all occasions, many more promises than are noted above. But it is these promises that connect us to God and assure us that we are loved. Consider using some of these promises during the construction process for your spiritual vision board, specifically during the affirmation process.

Chapter 5: How?

How to Create a Spiritual Vision Board that Works!

"For the Lord thy God hath blessed thee in all the works of thy hand."

Deuteronomy 2:7

When constructing a spiritual vision board that works, there are actually two different methods that you can use. The physical construction of a spiritual vision board can be described as a work of art of your own construction, examples of which you will see in the final chapter, or a digital version, which is easier for those of you who are comfortable using PowerPoint, InDesign, Photoshop, Canva, or another visual software platform; a few of these example you will also see in the final chapter.

Some of my workshop participants and students have shared how Pinterest is used to construct a digital version, such as the example to the left. Pinterest can also be paired with Canva to construct spiritual vision boards. Using the presentation option in Canva and the assortment of images in Pinterest provides depth and breadth to your spiritual vision board.

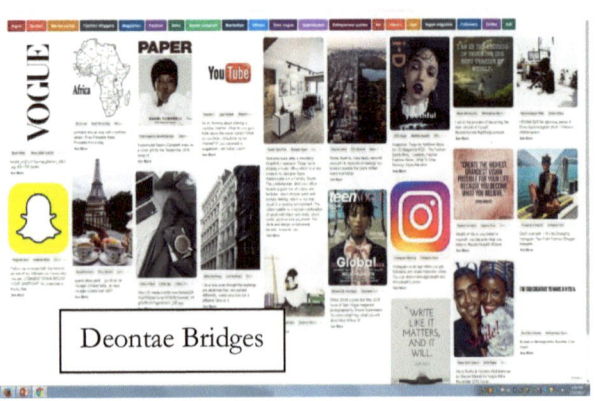

Deontae Bridges

In either case, I like the idea of using both a physical and a digital version. My physical spiritual vision board hangs on the wall over my desk in my office. Its placement makes it easy and convenient to walk into my office several times a day and meditate on its meaning. When I'm in the office, I can simply look up, and there it is. I make a practice of reciting the affirmations and mantras over and over again in my head when I'm not able to physically look at it. I appreciate the digital version more for its simplicity and aesthetic appeal. I just think that it's neater and prettier. All the images are clear, and the affirmations and mantras are color-coded. I've taken a picture of it with my cellphone and look at it often. I've saved it on the desktop of my computer, so whenever I'm on the computer (which is often), I can see it. And, finally, I think that it is easier to revise this version because images are more easily assessable through the internet. So, all I have to do is copy and paste a new image into the existing PowerPoint or Canva presentation. Whichever method you choose, you will easily be able to create your own by the simple, step-by-step process that is shared in this book.

In Chapter 3, a three-step process was noted. You will find this process below:

Step 1) Write down your vision clearly and plainly - ASK

Step 2) Use faith to activate your requests - BELIEVE

Step 3) Be prepared to take action through seeking and knocking – RECEIVE

However, when instructing the spiritual vision board workshops, I share that the construction process is actually four steps and not three. Here are those four steps:

1. ASK: Assemble your spiritual vision board with *intention*. Consider your prayer process in two parts: visual and verbal. Select specific pictures from various magazines that are *clear and plain*. These images will represent the visual part of your prayer request. Then develop affirmations, mantras, and motivational statements that reflect your selected images and support your vision. These verbal prayer requests should positively inspire and empower you.

2. BELIEVE: Having faith is more than just hoping for wishes to manifest themselves. We have to do our part by using faith-based conduits to secure our belief system. Inspired Thought (Spiritual Enlightenment), Visualization, Mindfulness, and Gratitude are all positive ways to activate your spiritual vision board and initiate your faith.

3. RECEIVE: Take action through seeking and knocking. Whatever we ask for, we can and will receive, but we need to do our part as co-creators. God is capable of giving us anything that our hearts desire, but in order to receive our blessings and physically take possession, we have to do our part. We need to take an active role by seeking for what we want – such as the new Lexus that I purchased to replace my Celica, or knocking on door after door until the one that God wants

us to walk through will open for us. In other words, we have to physically do our part to receive our blessing.

4. REVISE: Change your pictures/affirmations as you receive the desires of your heart. Acknowledge God's blessings by removing old prayer requests from your board in expectation of new blessings.

Please gather the following materials to complete your spiritual vision board:

- A foam board/poster board
- Various magazines
- Scissors
- Pen/Pencil
- Colored Markers/Paint
- Fabric to cover your board (optional)
- Scrapbook tape, two-sided tape, masking tape, or glue (some form of adhesive)
- Thumb tacks
- Picture of yourself (optional)

Let's Pray

FYI – sometimes it may be best to pray this prayer the night before you decide to begin your spiritual vision board, so that the Holy Spirit will have an opportunity to work with you and through you while you are sleeping. In any case, just remember to pray before you get started. Your prayer can be similar to the one noted below.

Father, thank you for this opportunity to develop a spiritual vision board that aligns with your purpose for my life. I ask that you guide me through this process. Allow the Holy Spirit to direct my path and enlighten my spirit. Help me to know what images I should gravitate to and use. Help me to develop specific affirmations, mantras, and motivational statements that will continue to help me grow and develop into the person that You want me to be. Thank you, Father and I ask these things in your son Jesus' name, Amen.

Chapter 6: Ask

ASK

Ask and it will be given to you, seek and you will find; knock and the door will be opened to you.
(Matthew 7:7)

The first step in our assembly process is to gather everything you need for your board in order to prepare yourself for asking. Your preparation also includes determining which type of spiritual vision board you are going to create (physical or digital). In Chapter 5, I have shared the basic difference between the two. But allow me to show you a few examples from my students.

Digital Examples

Brielle Callender
"I am now able to have major life events I want for myself in a visual display. I am now motivated and inspired to create the life I know I deserve."

Page | 57

Allison Wu

"I had so much fun learning about myself and where I stand in the fashion industry. Thank you Dr. Green Brown for your valuable lessons."

Physical Examples

Cierra Duval

"Creating the dream board was helpful to me because I could physically see and touch the aspects of my life I wanted to happen. Having a dream board put into perspective what my dreams, and aspirations are, and where I see myself achieving them. It let me dig deep inside into my desires and fears and create a vision of what I want my life to be. It put things into a positive perspective, and I believe my life has changed because of this."

Geornee Jefferies

"The dream board was an amazing project that opened my eyes to more jobs and careers. Before this class, I wanted to be a fashion stylist; now I know that I want to be a creative director and an inspirational role model to young girls and women of all races. Thank you Dr. Green Brown."

Have you made a decision? What type of spiritual vision board will you create?

Prepare For Asking

There are several ways to approach God and prepare oneself for asking. For we know that David asked of the Lord with a sincere heart and weepy posture. In Psalm 6:8-9, he said "the LORD hath heard the voice of my weeping. The Lord hath heard my supplication; the LORD will receive my prayer." In the multitude of ways that we can approach God and pray to Him, the best way is through our humility, having a pure, honest and open heart that seeks mercy, guidance and direction. We also must be clear and concise as we learned from Habakkuk 2:2 that when making our request known, these requests should be clear and plain.

SMART Plan

When making these requests, we need to be specific and intentional so that God knows that we are certain of our requests of Him. One of the best ways to ensure that our requests are clear and concise is to use the SMART plan. SMART stands for Specific, Measurable, Achievable, Realistic, and Time Sensitive. Both the visual component and the verbal component should follow the SMART plan. When applying the SMART plan, make sure that you can identify *specific* visual images that can be further detailed through your verbal mantras and motivational statements. For example, what make, model, color and features do you want in your new car? Make sure that you can *measure* the extent of your request. In other words, why ask for $100, when you know you really need $200. Do not put a limit on what God can do for you; know that there is no good thing that He would not give you (Psalm 84:11). Consider if these requests are actually *achievable*, some may seem challenging – but trust that we can do all things through Christ (Philippians 4:13). Please remember how important it is to be realistic, we can do all things through Christ, although some things may be a little beyond the scope of receiving. Finally make your requests *time sensitive*. If you need your electric bill paid tomorrow, remind God of the sense of urgency. Although He needs no reminders, He still desires our preciseness. Again, both the visual component and the verbal component should follow the SMART plan. Noted on the following pages of this chapter are further details of incorporating the SMART plan in your prayer requests.

1. **ASK**: Assemble your spiritual vision board with intention. The assembly process consists of developing a visual component as well as a verbal component. The visual component represents images that you are requesting of God: your goals, visions, dreams, and desires of heart expressed in vivid color and precise detail. Your verbal component consists of clearly written and developed affirmations, mantras, and motivational statements. These verbal requests usually directly support your visual images and are tailored to not only provide further details of your requests by using the SMART plan but also positively inspire and empower you.

You will need the following items for this step:
- A foam board/poster board
- Various magazines
- Scissors
- Pen/Pencil
- Colored Markers/Paint
- Fabric to cover your board (optional)
- Scrapbook tape, two-sided tape, masking tape, or glue (some form of adhesive)
- Thumb tacks
- Picture/Representation of Jesus (usually placed at the top of your board)
- Picture of yourself (optional – usually placed in the middle of your board)

Magazine Selection

Certainly, we all have our favorite magazines that we enjoy perusing from time to time, so you definitely want to use those magazines since they are plentiful, and you already have them around the house. However, there are other magazines that you don't read at all or perhaps less often. Therefore, you may want to pick up a few magazines of an assorted variety the next time you go to the drug store or grocery store, or you can ask some of your work colleagues to share with you some of the magazines that they are no longer reading. Request to borrow one or two the next time you have a doctor's appointment or consider having a spiritual vision board party at your home where you can invite friends and neighbors and share an assortment of magazines and other supplies. Creating your spiritual vision board in a group can be very beneficial. Since this process can be considered as a form of visual prayer, and we know when "two or three are gathered together in my name, there am I in the midst" (Matthew 18:20), imagine what could be produced from a group of believers who create their spiritual vision boards together.

The Awes Have it!

As you review each page of various magazines, you want to keep these things in mind. What is it that makes your spirit jump for joy? What makes your heart sing, with what images does your spirit connect spiritually and emotionally? Usually, when you are looking through some magazines that you are familiar with, you are somewhat desensitized by most of the images because you are used to seeing them. It may seem as if you have blinders on that prevent you from truly absorbing the level of engagement that can connect you to each image. However, this time I hope that your experience is different. Now that you have prayed about this process and your journey, it may be easier for you to view these images with a newfound appreciation. You may be able to view various images that ignite your spirit, images that you connect with on a deeper level, a spiritual level; it is these images that you want to use. Simply rip them or cut them out of the magazines and stack them until you are ready to use them.

Affirmation Confirmation

What are affirmations? Affirmations are positive phrases, statements, words and quotes that are written in first person and used to empower, encourage and overcome negative energy. To some extent, these affirmations give verbal meaning to your selected magazine images that you can further clarify when using the  SMART plan. Simply put, think about what your heart desires. Now ask for it by putting it in affirmation form clearly and specifically. Affirmations are the verbal part of your prayer experience. Let's review how you can develop your own affirmation statements.

Different Types of Affirmations

Usually, affirmation statements can be taken directly from scripture; however, some affirmations are not phrased exactly as we would see them in the Bible. In that case, it is perfectly natural to develop your own affirmation statement to address your specific desire. Some of the more popular affirmations begin with the following: I Am, I can, I feel, and I will. Let's review each one.

➢ **"I Am" Affirmations**

One of the most profound affirmations that you can use begins with "I Am". Taken from Exodus 3:14, God instructs Moses to use the phrase "I AM that I AM" as a response to those who inquire about who sent him to Egypt with the task of freeing the Israelites. God uses the words "I Am" to identify Himself. So when we use this phrase, we are not only identifying who we are, but we are also stating that God resides within us. For "greater is He who is in you" (1 John 4:4). In his book, *Wishes Fulfilled*, Dr. Wayne Dyer describes the "I Am" affirmation as an acceptance or knowing that God lives within us and that we are acknowledging our higher selves. And it is by our acknowledgement and the action that we take when operating in our higher selves that

God's promises can be manifested.

On the next page are some powerful "I Am" affirmations taken from scripture that you can include on your spiritual vision board.

- **"I Am" Affirmation Examples**
    - I am the righteousness of God in Jesus Christ (2 Corinthians 5:21).
    - I am the head and not the tail; I am above only and not beneath (Deuteronomy 28:13).
    - I am the light of the world (Matthew 5:14).
    - I am firmly rooted, built up, established in my faith and overflowing with gratitude (Colossians 2:7).
    - I am healed by the stripes of Jesus (Isaiah 53:5; 1 Peter 2:24).
    - I am greatly loved by God (Romans 1:7; Ephesians 2:4; Colossians 3:12; 1 Thessalonians 1:4).
    - I am strengthened with all might according to His glorious power (Colossians 1:11).
    - I am far from oppression, and fear does not come near me (Isaiah 54:14).

If we use scriptures as a guide, we can produce powerful affirmations. However, you can develop your own "I am" affirmations, such as those listed below; affirmations that are tailor-made to reflect your specific desires.

- I am strong.

- I am healthy, wealthy and blessed.
- I am at peace.

- **"I can" Affirmations**

What aspect in life would you like to change? The "I can" affirmations provide us with inspiration and motivation so that we can transition into what God has for us. Noted below are just a few "I can" affirmations noted in scripture, but keep in mind that you can also develop your own.

- **"I can" Affirmation Examples**
    - I can show God's kindness (2 Samuel 9:3).
    - With my God I can scale a wall (2 Samuel 22:30 & Psalm 18:29).
    - I can prevail (Proverbs 30:1).
    - I can speak freely (Acts 26:26).
    - I can do all this through him who gives me strength (Philippians 4:13).
- **"I feel" Affirmations**

The affirmation "I feel" is not as commonly used in scripture; however, you can develop your own positive affirmation statements such as the ones noted below.

- **"I feel" Affirmations Examples**
  - I feel healthy.
  - I feel at peace.
  - I feel joyful.
  - I feel great.

- **"I "have" Affirmations**

When using the affirmation "I have", think about those things that you desire to possess but currently are not tangible. So recognize that you have the power to turn situations around that have not occurred yet. And through your power of intention, you are intending those for things to come into fruition. A few scriptures that support the "I have" affirmation include:

- **"I have" Affirmation Examples**
  - I have found you righteous in this generation (Genesis 7:1).
  - I have found favor in your eyes; my Lord do not pass your servant by (Genesis 18:3).
  - I have done this with a clear conscience and clean hands (Genesis 20:5).

- The LORD, before whom I have walked faithfully, will send his angel with you and make your journey a success (Genesis 24:40).
- I will not leave you until I have done what I have promised you (Genesis 28:15).
- I have had a great struggle with my sister, and I have won (Genesis 30:8).
- I have promised to bring you up out of your misery (Exodus 3:17).
- I have given wisdom (Exodus 28:3).

Remember you can phrase the "I have" affirmations any way to best fit your needs or desires.

- **"I will" Affirmations**

The "I will" affirmation is mentioned quite a few times in the Bible when God shares His plans to complete a task. For example, in Genesis alone God states some of the following.

- **"I will" Affirmation Examples**
  - The Lord God said, it is not good for the man to be alone. I will make a helper suitable for him (Genesis 2:18).

  - I will remember my covenant between me and you and all living creatures of every kind (Genesis 6:18).

> To your offspring I will give this land (Genesis 24:7).

> I will make you into a great nation, and I will bless you; I will make your name great, and you will be a blessing (Genesis 12:2).

> The angel added, I will increase your descendants so much that they will be too numerous to count (Genesis 16:10).

Again, you can develop any "I will" affirmation that best fits your needs or desires. Now that you have a better understanding of how you can develop your affirmation statements, let's move on to the other verbal aspect of your spiritual vision board—mantras.

Mantras and Motivational Statements

Consider your verbal calling card. What would it say? How would you describe the *You* that you desire to be? Would it be a slogan or a bold word that commands a breakthrough of your mind, body and spirit? Mantras are simply motivational words or 2-3 word phrases that are similar to affirmations but can narrowly define who you are or desire to become. For example, maybe you feel confined. You could feel confined by your job, your family expectations, or physical/financial circumstance. When you think about getting away from it all to reenergize, the word *freedom* represents a great description of a new beginning. So, your mantra could be "Freedom." Or perhaps the mystery of what lies ahead unnerves you. Unexpected change does more than ruffle your feathers; change of any kind almost puts you in a chronic state of panic. In this case, a good mantra would reflect your ability to take on the world—fearlessly. So, your mantra could be "Fearless and Unshaken." You may wish to personalize it by stating your name then adding, "takes on the world" for example, "Lauren fearlessly takes on the world!" The word brave has also been used as a powerful mantra.

When formulating your motivational statement, this process can be very similar to that of composing affirmations and mantras, but these phrases are longer in length, usually at least a sentence; therefore, you have the opportunity to carefully construct what you would like to say. For example, one of my favorite motivational statements is "Be strong and of good courage." I remember the first time that I read this scripture from Joshua. In the first chapter, God actually repeats it, so when I read it the second time it was noted, and I could hear myself emphasizing it more. It was as though God was sharing with Joshua, *don't you know I got you; I will never leave you or forsake you. So be strong and of good courage, for I will always be with you.* I know that whatever we are going through, God is with us, and He will never leave us or forsake us.

My most recent motivational statement comes from Jabez' prayer to God where he requests that his territory is enlarged; I've phrased this motivational statement as follows: "Enlarge the territory of my service for you Lord." At the time that God placed it on my heart to include on my board, I truly didn't realize exactly what I was asking for. Since that initial request and my continued steadfastness in prayer, I have seen how God has begun to make changes in my life to afford me the time and commitment to take on this new role. Additionally, I've felt led to re-read the book by Bruce Wilkinson, *The Prayer of Jabez*. The first time I read it, I made a selfish connection to my dreams and aspiration. But now, not only have I found a new appreciation for the message that Wilkinson is sharing, but I also feel a connection to what God is preparing me for. I would encourage you to read *The Prayer of Jabez*, if you haven't already done so. Now take a moment to consider how you will develop your motivational statements.

How Affirmations and Mantras Work

In Romans 4:17, we are told to speak those things that are not as though they were. Notice the past tense used in this scripture. Our Kingdom operates on the premise that what you desire you already have, so we have to speak it or call it into existence. Our faith will act as a conduit to receive God's blessings.

Remember that we are made in the image of God; therefore, we possess the power to add intention to our destiny based on His laws. In the beginning, we learn in Genesis that God created the world and all that is contained within it based on saying, "Let there be…" and it was so.

We also must keep in mind that the power of life and death is in the tongue (Proverbs 18:21). Within this verse, we also learn that "for those who love it will eat its fruit." For those of us who recognize that our mouth can be our blessing or our curse, we must intentionally focus on always speaking positive statements and phrases. If we learn to use our mouth for good and learn to embrace the power of our words, then there is nothing that, through God, we cannot accomplish or achieve.

Our Subconscious at Work

To lend impact to our affirmations, mantras, and motivational phrases, each should be repeated over and over again with purpose and meaning. Through repetition, these words become subliminal messages to our brain. These messages act as a catalyst to our subconscious to change our thoughts and then parlay these thoughts into existence. It's similar to when we see a commercial advertising something appealing, such as a commercial for a pizza right around dinner time. The commercial entices us with the possibility of enjoying a nice hot, mouthwatering pizza that is loaded with cheese and all of our favorite fixings. Then, a minute later or less, we find ourselves ordering a pizza. Although the pizza commercial plays on our emotions—and perhaps weaknesses when it comes to a mouthful of delicious pizza—the act of repeating affirmations and mantras empowers us spiritually. We reconnect our brain to actions that produce positive outcomes. These outcomes come into fruition simply because we have spoken them into being.

Additional Assembling Tips

Now that you have selected your images, written affirmation statements and mantras, there are just a few more assembling tips that you need to know.

Coloring Your Spiritual Vision Board

The psychology of color dictates that all color evokes meaning and can be used as a nonverbal form of communication. Therefore, when we give color to our affirmations, mantras and motivational statements or phrases, each takes on a deeper and precise purpose. The depth of empowerment in purpose is due to the meaning behind the color that we have given it. The following colors can be used to reflect the following meanings:

- **Yellow** = joy, wisdom, happiness
- **Orange** = promotes creativity, optimism, and energy
- **Green** = health, growth, fertility, balance, and well being
- **Blue** = success, inspiration, loyalty, and faith
- **Purple** = leadership, royalty, luxury
- **Brown** = stability, and order
- **Pink** = relationships (romantic, family-oriented, friendship)

Assembling Your Spiritual Vision Board

Now that you have collected all your images, developed your affirmations, mantras, motivational statements and colorized them, you are ready to proceed with assembly. Before securing any of your images or verbal phrases to your board, you simply want to play around with the layout. Move your images and phrases in various positions on your board. Consider your prayer request as a priority list that you can position from the top to the bottom of your board. The desires that you want more would be placed closer to the top, and the other desires would be placed lower. This is not to say that the desires on the bottom are not important but think about a visit to your local grocery store. The grocer has deliberately placed more desirable items at eye level and arm's reach and less desirable items below. A similar strategy can be taken when identifying the most appropriate place to secure your images and phrases. Additionally, consider placing a photo of yourself or God (what represents God to you) in the center of your board. But remember what I said about priority and putting God first in everything. I, for example, have a picture of what God represents to me at the top of my board, and I have placed myself in the center. This step is optional, but some consider this step as an important aspect of defining your board. Then, once you have everything in place, you can secure the items with scrapbooking tape. I use colorful thumb pins that are easy to insert into a foam board and also easy to remove when changing out images. Select any adhesive you prefer.

Hang Your Spiritual Vision Board

Determine a spot in your home that you frequent often. Bedrooms and home offices are usually great locations. My physical spiritual vision board hangs over my desk in my home office. It's rather large in size—37x25 inches. When creating this board, I wanted to create one that was large enough to serve as a work of art and possibly take the place of a picture. Having the spiritual vision board in my home office serves two purposes. One, I'm in and out of my office several times a day, so when I walk in and head toward my desk, the spiritual vision board is one of the first things that I see. With the spiritual vision board constantly in view, I am able to focus on all or parts of it. I'm able to repeat the mantras and affirmations constantly and meditate on the images and visualize the outcome of promises that God has placed on my heart. Notice I mentioned visualize; we will cover this aspect more when we discuss Step 2 – Believe in Chapter 7.

Second, my home office is, for the most part, private. Therefore, everything in my office, including my spiritual vision board, is generally off limits to the public. Your spiritual vision board reflects *your* vision, not your best friend's, not your neighbor's, and not even your family's. That's not to say that any or all of these people cannot be included on your spiritual vision board if you desire. However, when God gave you your vision, He gave it to you and only you. You may want to think twice before sharing your intimate vision(s) with some people. Some may not understand or may not be supportive. Others may even find the whole idea of a spiritual vision board stupid. "As a man thinketh, so is he" (Proverbs 23:7). Everyone is entitled to his/her opinion about anything including the spiritual vision board. However, you do not want to allow other people's opinions to interfere with what God has placed on your heart or the vision that He has for you. Even believers may have a difficult time with what the spiritual vision board represents. Just consider this, as believers, we experience God differently. And God works with us and through us differently. So, although God is no respecter of persons (Acts 10:34), He treats us according to our level of faith and trust, however little or plentiful that is. Just how much do you believe in what God has for you? The next chapter shares with you just how important belief is when obtaining our hearts' desires.

Chapter 7: Believe

BELIEVE

Now faith is the substance of things hoped for, the evidence of things not seen (Hebrews 11:1).

When we believe for anything, we are hoping, wishing, and having faith in the fact that God really does answer prayer. But is our belief system one dimensional? In other words, what can we do with our faith to increase its level of intensity and demonstrate that we know God will provide us with the desires of our heart?

Step 2 of the spiritual vision board process spells out some of the steps that we can incorporate into our daily walk to activate the process and increase our belief system.

> BELIEVE: Use Faith, Inspired Thought (Spiritual Enlightenment), Visualization, Mindfulness, Gratitude, and Giving, to activate your spiritual vision board.

When I created my first vision board, I didn't take full advantage of this step; therefore, I was not able to reap the benefits that I had sown. And although God blessed me with some of my requests, those blessings were just a fraction of what He had in store for me.

Faith

Depending on what version of the Bible you read, you can find 300-400+ scriptures that reference faith, all of which address our ability to believe in something that may not be physically apparent, but deep down within us, we know that we know that we know there is a substance of truth. "Through faith we understand that the worlds were framed by the word of God, so that things which are seen were not made of things which do appear" (Hebrew 11:3). Although it's said that our faith can be as small as a mustard seed (Matthew 17:20), it could be said that those whose faith is more deeply developed, could be more likely to see their dreams come true, especially when they never give up or have doubt.

Hall of Faith

Although there are endless numbers of examples of those who were deeply committed to following the leadership and guidance of Jesus, not all of them are noted for using their faith to lead them to their destiny. In Hebrews 11: 4, we learn of these men and women with valor of faith who are noted in what most biblical scholars refer to as the Hall of Faith. You may be aware of some such as Noah who by faith built an ark to preserve all animals and mankind. Then there's Abraham and Sarah who by faith, even in their old age, were blessed with Isaac. Let's not forget Moses, who by faith led the Israelites to the Promised Land or Rahab who by faith did not perish when the walls of Jericho fell down. Although I did not mention all of the notables listed in the Hall of Faith, I do encourage you to read Hebrews 11 in its entirety before attempting to activate your spiritual vision board. This chapter may be very helpful to you to truly understand how you can unleash faith in your life.

Using Your Emotions to Activate Your Faith

In the movie *The Secret*, we learn how our actions, attitudes, and feelings play a role in our destiny and receipt of our blessings, how our appreciation for what we currently possess by giving thanks and showing gratitude can change our hearts and open doors of opportunity.

For example, after being underemployed for more than 2 years (32 months to be exact), I continued to remain hopeful. Even when I came close to receiving a job that I believed was my blessing, it appeared that every door I attempted to walk through would close for no apparent reason. But I still remained thankful. I thanked God for closing doors that He did not want me to walk through and opening doors that were more aligned with the purpose that He has for my life. Saying this is the easy part;

actually doing it, day after day, was a bit of a challenge. I received disappointment after disappointment, and it became harder to remain steadfast and hopeful. But I knew that, sometimes, when God desires to bless you with more than you can ever imagine or hope for, it is necessary to take you to another spiritual level—a level where He can bend you and shape you into what He wants you to be. But in order to reach that level, we must remain prayerful and "expect" a blessing. It is because we wait patiently and expectantly (Psalms 40:1; 42:5 & 11; 43:5; 103:5) that God opens doors.

What Do You Believe Is True?

Our perception of what we think is true creates our reality. It is these perceptions that shape our beliefs. Let's say, for example, that we believe in finding a mate. What would you do when you received him or her? How would having a mate alter your life? Perhaps you would have to set another place at the dinner table or make room in your closet and drawers. When you go to the movies, you are no longer sitting by yourself, but now you have someone beside you. In other words, your belief that you will receive your mate will alter your current lifestyle; therefore, you must begin to live according to the receipt of your blessing.

God didn't bless me with Randy until we were both in our late 40s. Perhaps that was for the best as we were both *extremely* ready to settle down and focus on building a life together. However, in preparation for my husband, I felt led to do the following. I first kept a journal of prayers that was about 2 pages long as a blessing to him, us, and our family. I asked God to keep us healthy, wealthy and blessed; to make sure we were equally yoked, compatible, and faithful. I described my husband in full detail. I prayed about our home, finances, and so much more. This vision of a mate occurred years before I developed the spiritual vision board. But once the spiritual vision board was developed, it took my vision to the next level. When I had dinner, I set a place at the table for him. When I went to bed, his spot was to my left, next to the door. When I went anywhere alone, I would leave enough space to accommodate him in my car.

When Randy and I first met, he shared with me that he believed God brought us together. I will admit that there have been times when I had doubts. Like any relationship, we have had our tough times. However, as tough as it got, we both realized that our belief in God and what He has blessed us with will not always be a joyride, but the love that we share is undeniable, and our trust in God shapes our depth of believing.

Spiritual Enlightenment

Now knowing and acknowledging that you should wait expectantly for your blessings, the next aspect that you need to keep in mind to bring your prayer request into fruition occurs through *spiritual enlightenment*, or as Jack Canfield described in the movie *The Secret* inspired thought. Spiritual Enlightenment (Inspired Thought) occurs when you suddenly become enlightened with a specific idea that directs you to obtain what you have prayed for and released or surrendered to God. This enlightenment process may not occur immediately. For Canfield, it took about a month after he prayed about earning

$100,000 in one year. The result? He became the best-selling co-author of *Chicken Soup for the Soul* and earned $92,000. Ok, so I know what you're thinking. He received slightly less than what he asked for. But he didn't complain. In fact, he went through the vision process again but this time requesting a million dollars. The first royalty check that his publisher ever wrote was for a million dollars, and needless to say, it was to Canfield for *Chicken Soup for the Soul*.

Moments of inspired thought and spiritual enlightenment can occur at any time. For Canfield, this moment of inspiration occurred when he was relaxing in the shower. Consider when you are most relaxed or at ease. Is it in the shower or bath? Perhaps when you are praying or mediating. Some of my visions have occurred on the cusp of being awake and transitioning from a deep sleep. Inspired thought can occur in a number of different ways, such as the following:

- **When you are relaxed.**
  - In the shower, right before you go to bed, or before you wake in the morning.
- **When you are discussing a situation** (brain storming) with friends, co-workers, etc.
- **When you are energized.**
  - Exercising, cooking, simply doing something that you're passionate about.
  - When you are in the moment, when your will aligns with God's will, He is present and the Holy Spirit is communicating with you.

During mindfulness: some describe inspired thought as a byproduct of mindfulness because during that time you are fully conscious and engaged in the present; therefore, the Holy Spirit is more likely to share wisdom with you, and you are more prone to hear and receive it.

You can literally receive a vision, an idea, an inspired thought, perhaps even a still, small word of encouragement, motivation, or direction anytime and anywhere. But whenever you receive that message, take it seriously and act on it. Because it is in that moment that God is directing your path and guiding you towards doors that you should walk through to receive all that He has for you.

Visualize

When we visualize, we live in the moment of receiving our blessing. While meditating on the images, affirmations, mantras, and motivational statements on our spiritual vision boards, we experience all the joy, happiness, and sense of accomplishment that we have expected. The practice of visualization extends our levels of faith and expectation. It signifies to God that, not only are we waiting patiently and expectantly, but we can imagine how our lives will change once we receive the desires of our hearts. As with any of the other steps in this process, visualization needs to be repeated often enough that you remain hopeful, but if your emotions falter, and visualizing becomes more of a chore than a joy, don't do it. Our positive attitudes will bring on the change that we are waiting for. Remember the joy of the Lord is your strength (Nehemiah 8:12).

Give to Others

When I first read Deepak Chopra's *The Seven Spiritual Laws of Success*, the mix of emotions was overwhelming, and I wanted to do everything that he talked about right away. However, one law that was extremely easy to seamlessly incorporate into my daily life was the law of giving. As Chopra describes it, the law of giving is a universal exchange of dynamic energy, "Our willingness to give that which we seek (provides us with an opportunity to) keep the abundance of the universe circulating in our lives" (p. 25). In other words, in order to receive, we must be cognizant of giving. And when we give specifically what we desire, we are more likely to receive it.

The dynamic exchange of circulation that Chopra addresses tells us that we should remain open to keep the circulation process of giving and receiving constantly flowing. Once we cut it off by not giving, this in turn limits or stifles our ability to receive. In Luke 6:38, we learn that if we "give, it shall be given unto you; good measure, pressed down, shaken together, and running over." As I mentioned, this law is probably the easiest one to incorporate because when we are around others, we are given several opportunities daily to meet each other's needs. And these needs often do not cost us anything. Our gift to someone else could be in the form of a compliment, well wishes or even a prayer. Sometimes all people may need is an encouraging word. No man or woman is an island; one of our purposes in life is to help others. Chopra ends this chapter on the law of giving by sharing 3 simple ways to implement it; noted below is just one of those ways:

Today I will gratefully receive all the gifts that life has to offer me. I will receive the gifts of nature: sunlight and the sound of birds singing, or spring showers or the first snow of winter. I will also be open to receiving from others, whether it be in the form of a material gift, money, a compliment, or a prayer.

Be Thankful

If we truly believe that God will bless us with the desires of our heart, then we need to thank Him for all our blessings. Again, consider that you have already received what you have been praying for. What is the natural thing to do when someone gives you something or does something for you—thank them, right?

Put yourself in that moment of receipt, and simply begin to thank God for all that He has done for you in addition to what He is doing. You are acknowledging that your blessing is on the way, and you are ready to receive it. In 1 Thessalonians 5:18, we are told to "Be thankful in all circumstances" and Ephesians 5:20 states, "Giving thanks always for all things unto God and the Father in the name of our Lord Jesus Christ."

When we give thanks, we demonstrate to God that we have a grateful heart, a heart that is open to receive all His loving kindness. Even when we experience trials and tribulations, we need to share with Him that we may not necessarily be thankful for the current situation, but, because we rely and depend on Him, we can be thankful that He will comfort us and provide us with all that we need during our times of struggle. He will give us provisions during our time of lack. So, consider being thankful during the tough times, but expectantly wait for God's blessing to come through for you. Romans 12:12 asks for us to experience "rejoicing in hope; patient in tribulation; continuing instant in prayer."

Before bedtime, when I say my nightly prayers, I try to make a habit each night of giving thanks. I give thanks for the wonderful relationships He's given me, for my home, health, means of employment, the list goes on and on. When I was underemployed for 32 months, certainly I felt a level of frustration, and there were times when I wondered if God actually heard me, listened to me and cared about my need to be financially independent. But I still thanked Him, knowing that He would not let me down. I thanked Him for keeping me through the 32 months of underemployment. I thanked Him for Randy's love, support and patience, and simply hanging in there with me as I applied for job after job, hoping and praying for a change. I thanked Him for giving me provisions during my time of trial. I thanked Him for my new job that was specifically designed for me. I thanked Him for closing doors that He did not want me to walk through and for opening doors of opportunity that He specifically developed for me.

Close to the end of my receiving a new position, God placed it on my heart to put the following affirmation on my spiritual vision board. It reads, "I am thankful, fulfilled, appreciated, and highly compensated for using my gifts in my careers." I'm not sure exactly how many months after that affirmation was placed on my board that I landed the full-time consulting position working with doctorate students who are completing their dissertations. After accepting that position, one of my former bosses offered me an adjunct professor position at the university where she was currently employed. At first, I didn't really want another teaching position, but once I learned of the compensation, and that it would more than double what I was currently making at my other teaching position, I was reminded of what I prayed for—"highly compensated." Needless to say, I accepted the position. A year later, I was promoted from adjunct to a full-time teaching position and was able to quit my part time jobs.

Giving thanks may be one of the last steps to include during the second step of "Believe"—but it certainly is one of the most important. Some common practices to keep in mind when following the Believe step include:

> ➢ Recognize that your faith can be as small as a mustard seed

- But the deeper your faith (*Hall of Faithers*), the bigger your blessings
- Know what you believe in is TRUE.
- Activate this process through spiritual enlightenment.
- Visualize that you have achieved what you have asked for.
  - Consider your images, affirmations, mantras and motivational statements then LIVE in that moment of receiving your blessing.
  - Repeat your affirmations, mantras and motivational statements as you visualize a new and improved you.
- Visualize that your gift (blessing) is ready for you to open.
  - Take on the emotions that you would like to experience.
  - Physically act out your reaction to the receipt of your blessings, and then use this experience as a guide to visualize your response over and over again.
- Keep the dynamic energy of giving and receiving circulating.
- Give thanks for all that He has done, and all that He is doing.
- Remain in this constant space of thankfulness and mindfulness.

Next, we come to the good part—Receive!

Chapter 8: Receive

RECEIVE

For everyone who asks receives; the one who seeks finds; and to the one who knocks, the door will be opened.
(Matthew 7:8)

The next step in the receipt of your blessings is realizing that once you have asked God for something and you believe, you then must accept it by physically taking it. However, let me share that there is a difference between *getting* and *receiving*. Getting occurs when we conduct works of the flesh to obtain what we want, but not what God wants for us. Receiving occurs when we accept the gifts that God is blessing us with. Your gift isn't yours until you take possession of it. Furthermore, God usually expects us to do our part in order for Him to do His part.

Step 3. RECEIVE: Be prepared to take action through seeking and knocking.

In order to receive your blessing, you must physically take possession of it. Receiving anything takes on a physical responsibility on your part. If someone knocks on your door, then you must physically answer it if you are interested in receiving company. Some may wonder who wouldn't accept a gift or blessing from God. If everyone was so willing to take possession of what God has blessed us with, it would not have been necessary to devote close to 40 scriptures on taking possession. In Deuteronomy, we find most of these scriptures. During this time, the Israelites are close to the end of their 40-year journey. And God has blessed them with their land of milk and honey—the Promised Land. Consider this scripture from Deuteronomy 11:9-12 on taking possession.

> *And so that you may live long in the land the Lord swore to your ancestors to give to them and their descendants, a land flowing with milk and honey. The land you are entering to take over is not like the land of Egypt, from which you have come, where you planted your seed and irrigated it by foot as in a vegetable garden. But the land you are crossing the Jordan to take possession of is a land of mountains and valleys that drinks rain from heaven. It is a land the Lord your God cares for; the eyes of the Lord your God are continually on it from the beginning of the year to its end.*

Another excellent scripture on taking possession is noted in 1 Kings 21:15, that shares "Take possession of the vineyard of Naboth the Jezreelite."

Go and Receive

In 1Samuel 23:4, we learn that David inquired of God about his battle with the Philistines. And God replied, "Go down to Keilah, for I am going to give the Philistines into your hand." So, David and his men went to Keliah, fought the Philistines and carried off their livestock. He inflicted heavy losses on the Philistines and saved the people of Keilah.

Notice in this scripture the word *Go* and, in response, David *went*. In order for David to receive God's blessing, he needed to take action. Our physical response to God's gifts indicates that we acknowledge and receive whatever God has for us. God asks us to wait for the desires of our heart, but during this waiting process, we should expect to be blessed.

Touch and Be Healed

Another example can be found in Mark 5:25-34, where we learn of a woman who had bled for 12 years. Although several doctors tried to cure her, she continued to suffer and spent all that she had. But she knew that if only she had the chance to touch His clothes, she would be healed. Immediately, upon the touch of the hem of His cloak, the bleeding stopped, and she was healed. God responded to the woman with these words: "Daughter, your faith has healed you. *Go* in peace *and be freed* from your suffering."

Rise and Walk

This final example comes from John 5:5-8, of a man who had been paralyzed for 38 years. He heard about the healing pool of Bethesda that was touched by an Angel of God every year to heal believers of their aliments. It is said that multiple people would visit the pool yearly to be healed of conditions ranging from paralysis to blindness, but only the first to enter the pool would receive the healing. The paralyzed man tried and tried for years to get close enough to enter the pool but could not. Jesus saw this man and asked him, "Do you want to be made well?" Now listen to how the paralyzed man responded. Instead of simply saying, "Yes, Lord, heal me," he opted to provide an excuse for why he was not able to receive his blessing. "Sir, I have no man to put me into the pool when the water is stirred up; but while I am coming, another steps down before me." How often have you been within arm's reach of your blessing, and instead of taking it, you found a reason not to? How often have you thought, *Boy wouldn't it be nice if...* and then considered all the reasons why you shouldn't or looked for excuses not to receive what's is intended for you? That is exactly what this man did. He was already there, and he had been there for years; so other than his paralysis, could it be that excuses can produce such a stronghold that he missed out on a life changing blessing?

When we interfere with what is in line for us to receive, and we also allow others or excuses to interfere with what God has in store for us, we simply miss out on an opportunity to be blessed. But sometimes God takes mercy on us and intervenes. This is what happened to the paralyzed man. God was merciful and patient with this man and his excuses. He simply replied, "*Rise*, take up your bed and walk." And immediately the man was made well, took up his bed, and walked.

The reality is if you want something bad enough, you will do whatever it takes to receive it. And sometimes that means not allowing others to get in the way of your blessing. Someone shared with me long ago that other people's motives are very seldom unselfish. In other words, most people are always thinking and looking for opportunities to benefit themselves, not necessarily what would benefit someone else. So, if that is the case, then you always have to be ready to politely step up and take hold of what God has intended for you. Because if you don't, there will always be someone else who patiently and expectantly will take what you have neglected to receive.

So, I'll close this chapter by asking, now that you are aware that receiving is a physical response to prayer, how will you respond to the blessing that God has prepared for you?

Chapter 9: Revise

REVISE

Review the past for me (Isaiah 43:26)

The final step is a call to action. This step provides an opportunity for us to reflect and review God's blessings as we begin to revise our spiritual vision boards in anticipation of new blessings.

Step 4 REVISE: Revise pictures, affirmations, mantras and motivational statements as you receive your blessings. Revision of your spiritual vision board is probably the easiest step to complete, primarily because you are in a positive space, a space of thankfulness and gratitude, so it may be easy for you to reflect on all that God has done; therefore, the first thing that you should do, if you haven't done it already, is to thank God.

➢ Show your GRATITUDE by thanking GOD for His blessing.

Acknowledge that without Him, you cannot achieve His will and receive His grace, mercy and blessings. Let God know that your heart is filled for all that you've received. King David shares his heart-filled devotion to God throughout the book of Psalms. One of those devotions is located in Chapter 107 where he describes why he is so thankful to God.

> *Give thanks to the LORD, for he is good;*
> *his love endures forever.*
> *Let the redeemed of the LORD tell their story—*
> *those he redeemed from the hand of the foe,*
> *those he gathered from the lands,*
> *from east and west, from north and south.*
> *Some wandered in desert wastelands,*
> *finding no way to a city where they could settle.*
> *They were hungry and thirsty,*
> *and their lives ebbed away.*
> *Then they cried out to the LORD in their trouble,*
> *and he delivered them from their distress.*
> *He led them by a straight way*
> *to a city where they could settle.*
> *Let them give thanks to the LORD for his unfailing love*
> *and his wonderful deeds for mankind,*
> *for he satisfies the thirsty*
> *and fills the hungry with good things.*

Admittedly, we all are not quite as eloquent as King David; however, God does not expect us to be. God simply wants us to acknowledge what He has done for us and in our lives and thank Him for it. Then you can move forward with your revisions.

Dead Prayer

There are times when you may have asked God for the same thing repeatedly. We may even ask God during our moment of doubt – "Why have You not blessed me with what I've asked?" There could be two reasons why you have not received your request: 1) it is not your season (time) to receive it. In Ecclesiastes 3:1, we learn that "There is a time for everything, and a season for every activity under the heavens." For example, when I asked God for my husband, I asked Him what felt like a billion times at least. But His response was not no, it was not yet. There were aspects in my life that I believe I needed to focus on while I was single. But as soon as I accomplished those tasks, Randy showed up and the rest is history – or he is now my husband.

2) God may not bless you with your request because of a phrase that He shared with me somewhat recently. It is called *dead prayer*. Dead prayer means that you are asking for something in vain. The request does not align with God's plans or purpose for your life. This misalignment could mean that He has something so much better for you, but you do not realize how HUGE He would like to bless you. Again, the scripture of Jeremiah 29: 11-13 comes to mind:

"For I know the plans I have for you" declares the Lord, "plans to

prosper you and not to harm you, plans to give you hope and a future. Then you will call on me and come and pray to me, and I will listen to you. You will seek me and find me when you seek me with all your heart."

The best example that I can share about the concept of dead prayer is a dollar amount that I've had on my spiritual vision board ever since I started conducting workshops. I have not received that specific amount, and when I asked God about it, He shared the concept of dead prayer and then went on to say that I was limiting my request. I cannot imagine what God has for me monetarily, but I do not limit His ability to give me His best.

Update your spiritual vision board by creating new goals/affirmations.

Before you update your spiritual vision board, you have to remove the original images and affirmations that God has already blessed you with. Sure, you can toss these former blessings away, but consider gathering them and placing them in a scrapbook that you can revisit occasionally and reflect on. For those of you who journal, it would be easy to add this step into your journaling process. If not, it may not be too challenging to consider developing a scrapbook for that purpose. Every time you revisit your collection of former images and affirmations, a blanket of gratefulness will overcome you. You'll reflect and reminisce about the time when your blessing occurred and the journey you experienced to receive it. This reflection process will help you with the last thing that you will do in revising your spiritual vision board.

When you're constantly in a space of thankfulness, a peace like no other overcomes you. It's during those times that God shares with you more of His will and *His will* then become a desire of *your heart*. What are those desires you may ask? What is the next step that God desires for you to adventure upon? When you revisit how you originally created your spiritual vision board, these questions will become clear. You will repeat the image gathering process. Find pictures that reflect your desires. Develop affirmation statements that reflect those images. Develop new mantras. Then place images, affirmations and mantras on your existing spiritual vision board. The cycle repeats itself each and every time God blesses you, and you acknowledge His goodness.

We've now come close to the end of our spiritual vision board journey. You are more informed about what a spiritual vision board is, how it works, and how to construct it using the 4 simple steps detailed in the previous chapters. But when is the best time to begin this process? When should you consider developing your own spiritual vision board?

Chapter 10: When?

When is the Best Time to Create a Spiritual Vision Board?

WHEN

In the beginning (Genesis 1:1)

The best time to start anything should always be at the beginning or firsts. When are you most likely to complete an important task on your to-do list? Usually, most people like to start their day doing something productive, or simply getting it out of the way, so that they do not have to be concerned with it later. Although I'm not much of a morning person, I still prioritize my mornings by checking things off of my mental to-do-list, based on all the things that I plan to accomplish first thing in the morning.

First things First

Completing your spiritual vision board should take on the idea of being first. For example, the beginning of a New Year is optimal. Instead of creating another list of resolutions that you're not even sure you can keep during the year, start developing your spiritual vision board as a visual prayer, and list the personal and professional goals that you need God's help to complete.

But before you begin this new venture, I suggest that you pray for guidance, spiritual enlightenment, and alignment with God's plans for your life first. Best case scenario pray the night before so that while you're sleeping, visions and words of enlightenment can enter your dreams. You may not recall everything that you dreamt about, but The Holy Spirit will remind you as you peruse various pictures in magazines. The Holy Spirit will also help to guide you to develop affirmations, mantras, and motivational statements that best reflect God's plan for your life. So do not forget to pray first before you actually begin.

Spring as a New Beginning

When we think about seasonal beginnings, spring best represents a fresh start. It is not uncommon for many to associate spring with rebirth, renewal, and the resurrection. This sense of renewal is expressed in one of author Robert Orben's quotes that states, "Spring is God's way of saying, one more time!" For after months of the cold wintry months, spring provides hope and rejuvenation as the cold crisp days of past thaw to a one more time experience, expressed by the warmth of the morning sun that provides an inviting reawakening.

Our fur-covered friends emerge from hibernation. Rain showers douse the dry stiff ground, giving life to blossoming flowers and budding trees. Birds fill the air with joyful song. When we think about spring holidays and celebration, environmentalists support the preservation of our planet through Earth Day, and Christians partake in one of the most sacred days of remembrance and celebration – Easter.

So, consider the spring as another opportunity to start anew. You can either revise your existing spiritual vision board or take advantage of this new seasonal beginning to start your first spiritual vision board.

Where Should I Start?

If you are hesitant to begin, just consider what God has placed in your heart. Then think about what you would also like to accomplish both personally and professionally. You could even start with the simple task of writing all of your desires down on a piece of paper (write down your vision and make it plain (Habakkuk 2:2); that way, your spiritual mind will already be in a mindset of completing all that God has for you to accomplish. Once you begin searching through magazines for your images, you will be amazed at how certain pictures will begin to leap out at you. Such images will tug at your heart and your spirit through a divine connection. You will find new meaning and purpose to your life.

Other Opportunities to Start Boarding

There are additional opportunities for you to think about firsts or beginnings. If you are reading this book for the first time and it is not the beginning of a New Year or spring, consider how beginnings could also start with each month, each week, and each day. Take advantage of the sacredness associated with beginnings. For we learn in Genesis 1:1 that "In the beginning God created the heavens and the earth." Some may say, "Well, that's the Old Testament," which is true, but in the New Testament, John 1:1-5, we learn:

In the beginning was the Word, and the Word was with God, and the Word was God. He was with God in the beginning. Through him all things were made; without him nothing was made that has been made. In him was life, and that life was the light of all mankind. The light shines in the darkness, and the darkness has not overcome it.

We also learn (in Ezra 7:9) that he (Ezra) began his journey from Babylon on the first day of the first month then continued his journey reaching Jerusalem on the first day of the fifth month, which was in accordance with the good hand of God upon him. All that we are and all that God has for us are within our reach; it is only up to us to accept it. Remember, by accepting our blessings, we become an active participant in all that God has for us. So, what are you planning to do this New Year, this spring or at the beginning of each month, week or day? I have a good idea where you can start. You also want to think about the sacredness associated with "first". Proverbs 3:9-10 shares with us to "Honor the Lord with your wealth, with the first fruits of all your crops; then your barns will be filled to overflowing, and your vats will brim over with new wine." It's so important to keep God first in all we do, for then He will bless us more abundantly than we could ever imagine.

Final Thoughts

Creating a spiritual vision board that works can be a rewarding and spiritually fulfilling process when we consider using a vision board as *a visual form of prayer*. As noted earlier on in this book, you certainly don't have to create a spiritual vision board in order to receive all that God has for you. But when we consider our private and most sacred time with our Father, having a physical tool that we can look at, engage with, and that will help us to savor the intimacy in knowing just how much He loves us can be a priceless experience. One of my favorite scriptures (1 Corinthians 2:9) addresses how we really don't know what God has in store for us:

What no eye has seen,
what no ear has heard and
what no human mind has conceived
the things God has prepared for those who love him—
these are the things God has revealed to us by his Spirit.

It's important that you know just how much God intends to bless you and give you more than you could ever imagine. And He will! So, I pray that God will continue to bless you and your journey through using the spiritual vision board as a visual form of prayer; now you are better equipped to develop one that really works.

May God Bless You Always,

Dr. Cris

Chapter 11: Spiritual Vision Board Examples

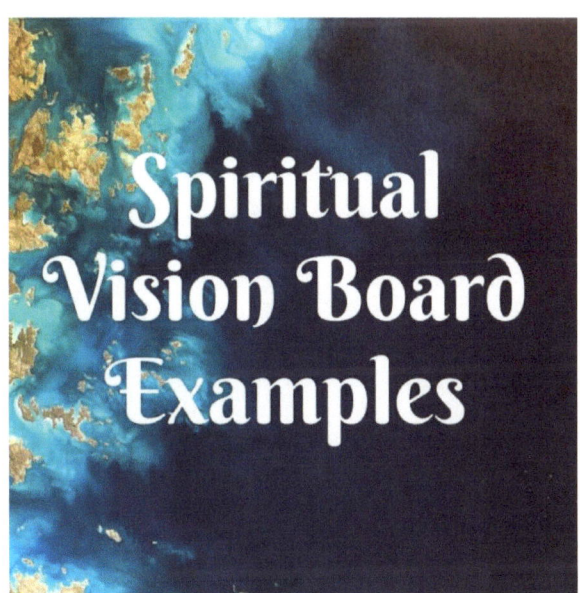

Thanks to the wonders of social media, this large world that we live in has become smaller and more connected. With such platforms as Instagram, Facebook, Pinterest, and Twitter, we can appreciate others' photos, videos inspiration quotes, and yes—spiritual vision boards. During the process of writing and researching this book, God shared with me how He is using other (spiritual) vision board coaches like myself to understand His promises and transform the lives of so many who are praying for a change in their lives. This next section is a tribute to some of those spiritual vision board coaches, some spiritual vision board users, and their testimonies to how using a spiritual vision board as a visual form of prayer has changed their lives.

Enjoy!

Alicia Domico is a (spiritual) vision board coach from Cleveland, Ohio. Alicia shares her story in her own words. "I have been on a spiritual journey over the last 3 years that has led me to be a (Spiritual) Vision Board Coach. Through my own experiences, I have realized that I have gifts to share with the world and that connecting to the spiritual energy within me and within the soul of others is why we are here. It's the experiences of life that teach us the lessons we are to learn to help open our hearts and free our minds from any form of fear and discover the freedom and love that already exists within us. Within each lesson, experience or situation we face in life, we can find the blessing that we are given when our hearts are fully open to receive them. That is the journey of the soul. I have found (Spiritual) Vision Boards

Alicia Domico
Spiritual Vision Board Coach

have helped me connect with that part of me that is free from limitation, lack and fear that have been part of my conditioning over the course of my life. "Boarding" to me is about setting intentions out into the universe through words, phrases and images and having those positive intentions vibrate back to me and create my realities. "Boarding," to me, is about being in the present moment with that part of me that knows the truth about my desires, dreams and wants. When you can be with your board in the present moment and use it as a way for the Divine to express through your heart onto the board, you open your heart up to receive the abundance that is your birthright. Once my boards are complete, I always take a few moments each day and meditate on what the words, phrases and images mean to me and feel them vibrate through my body. By doing this daily, I am sending these feelings out into the universe to come back to me, and I trust that what will come back is better than I could imagine myself. Each time I do this with an open heart, I am amazed at what is shown to me."

"As a (Spiritual) Vision Board Coach, my desire is to help others find or ignite a spark within themselves that will help set their minds free of fear, lack and limitations. I have seen amazing results in increased creativity, harmonious relationships, increased health and overall focus and awareness. On the next few pages, enjoy some of my clients' boards and testimonies."

"I have it (spiritual vision board) in my bedroom so that when I wake up, I see my dream. Alicia did such a great job guiding me to create the vision I wanted, it was like she could read my mind. Being able to look at your dream in pictures and words is empowering and motivating. It gives you a sense of pride within yourself and the nudge to move forward. All the barriers you put in front of yourself start to seem ridiculous and not barriers at all. The workshop transformed the way I look at the world and gave me the confidence I needed to keep chasing my dreams."

Lisa Franklin is an Assistant Director of Programs & Research at Cleveland State University

"Alicia's (Spiritual) Vision Board Workshop is an effective way for adults to gain an understanding of their inner workings and potentially resolve unknown issues about whatever topic the creator of the board has in mind. For me, I was focused on my business and was surprised at the results of the board, which has had me reflecting on my true goals. This is a great alternative to corporate team-building exercises."

Dr. Karen Gurney- CEO of Career IQ

"Alicia's (Spiritual) Vision Board Workshop renewed a desire to have (Spiritual) Vision Boards as a tool for achieving my life goals. She helped me see that my (spiritual) vision board should focus on how I want to feel, not just on things that I want. Her meditative creative process as well as her instructions for additional work after the board was created have had a tremendous effect on my everyday life. Intentions are a powerful tool, and a few days after this workshop, I began to experience the desired results I had envisioned and placed on my board."

Alexis Jones, Product Support Specialist for Streamlink Software

Alicia Domico

Alicia Domico

Alicia Domico

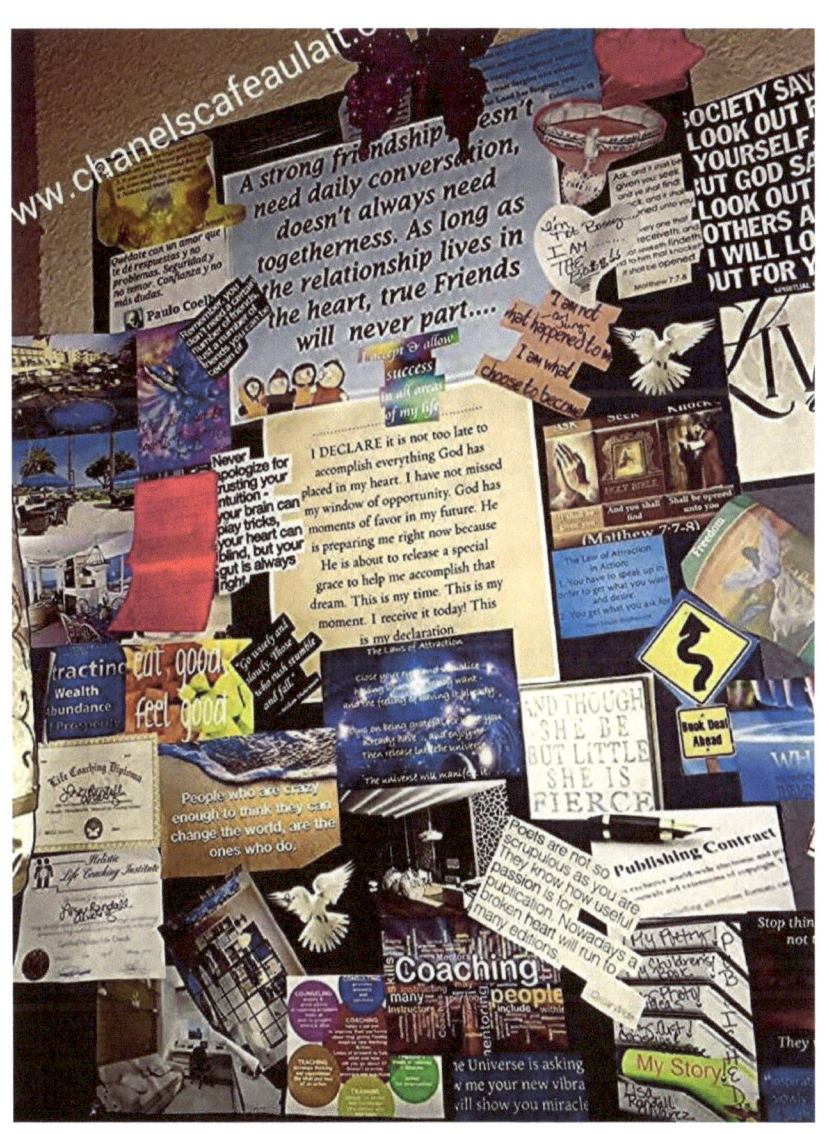

Lisa Alvarez

Lisa Alvarez has also helped others in their journey to transition using the (spiritual) vision board as an Empath, Certified Life Coach, Vision Board Coach, Law of Attraction Practitioner, writer, poet, entrepreneur, philanthropist, wife, and mother to four fantastic children. As a Certified Life Coach, Lisa specializes in relationship coaching, building self-esteem, and assisting others with removing mental blocks to happiness. It is her passion in life to help others realize their God- given gifts and purpose; to build confidence, and remove those nagging self-doubts. As a Law of Attraction Practitioner and (Spiritual) Vision Board Coach, her goal is to assist others in creating the life they deserve through the assistance of visualization and the teachings of Universal Laws. A California native and lover of nature, she can often be found strolling along the beach... (Her personal favorite is Half Moon Bay).

Lisa Alvarez
Spiritual Vision Board Coach

In Lisa's words: "I began this journey in June of 2014, after three of my four children moved out of our home. It occurred to me that I needed some direction when I felt that nagging (almost) empty nest feeling... I kept thinking, *What is my purpose after mom and wife? Who am I? What am I here to accomplish? What is God's plan for me now? WHAT IS MY PURPOSE?* Then I discovered the Law of Attraction...

Things began to change significantly after that! One afternoon, while browsing the Internet for inspiration, I discovered a video on YouTube about (Spiritual) Vision Boards... This intrigued me so much that I immediately sat down and made some strong goals for myself. Not too long after, I made my first board. My (Spiritual) Vision Boards allowed me to use The Law of Attraction to its fullest potential. I have literally created my future, right before my eyes. My goals of becoming a Certified Life Coach and an LOA Practitioner in addition to starting my own business, Chanel's Café Au Lait for Lisa Alvarez INC., have all come to fruition. I have made new friends. My connection to God and Source has strengthened. I am on my way to being a published author and motivational speaker. What is next on my agenda? The Universe is Infinite… And so are the possibilities! In closing, I would like to leave you with this absolute truth: Visualization tools are definitely a Godsend… The idea of (Spiritual) Vision Boards is given to us from Source for us to use to achieve our wildest dreams. There is nothing in this world you cannot accomplish when you put your mind to it! ASK, BELIEVE, AND RECEIVE!"

Lisa Alvarez

Lisa's daughter, Emiliana Alvarez

Susanne Calman

"I discovered the beauty of (spiritual) vision boards at a time in my life when I was burnt out with being way too responsible for family and business. My first (spiritual) vision board blew my mind – who knew I wanted to sell my yoga centre, host my own retreats and learn French? I didn't….but my soul did! I listened and acted upon the wisdom I had been shown. I now include (Spiritual) Vision Boards on my retreats because they allow a woman to remember what nourishes and feeds her body, mind, heart and soul.

Susanne Calman
Spiritual Vision
Board Coach

Sometimes it's a big wake-up call, and other times it's a gentle reminder from her spirit. (Spiritual) Vision Boards are a gentle and loving way to reconnect to your feminine spirit and remember what/who ignites your creativity, inspiration, freedom, joy, peace + passion for life + love so that you can bring more of these into your life."

www.femininespirit.com.au

Susanne Calman

Johannah Barton
Confetti Design

Linda Kropich

Cherisa Allen
Spiritual Vision Board Coach

Cherisa Allen is a proud native of Ypsilanti, Michigan. As the oldest of eight children, she learned at an early age the importance of both family and the teachings of the Holy Spirit. Cherisa was very active in school, in church and her community that have continued into her adult life. She is a proud graduate of Eastern Michigan University, completing both her bachelor's and master's degree.

Cherisa is devoted to making changes and transforming lives of women everywhere. She is a published author; *Revelation, Resignation, Restoration*. She is the Owner of Do You See What I See, LLC? She is a Motivation/Inspiration Speaker and a Transformational Life Coach. Cherisa tackles tough issues that inhibit women from living productive and healthy lives. She is committed to educating them on how to become strong, independent, and loving women.

Cherisa's shares the following in her own words, "work with (spiritual) vision boards has opened new and diverse doors for women to walk through. My (spiritual) vision board workshops have brought a newfound meaning to *writing the Vision and making it Plain*. Women come in the workshop not knowing what to expect and leave with an understanding that they are truly the Captain of their ships…sailing wherever they dream of. After adapting, Dr. Cris' foundation for teaching spiritual vision boards I have not only grown and gained an understanding of what God has for us, but also realize that no force on earth can take it away. I've learned how important it is to also inspire women to continue to create and add to their (spiritual) vision boards, watching and waiting with great anticipation of what will manifest if they intentional trust the process God has prepared for them. Finally, I remind each woman I encounter that… it is up to each of us to Trust and believe that when God gives us a vision, He provides provision.

Trust in the Lord with all thine heart; lean not to thy own understanding, in all thy ways acknowledge Him and He shall direct thy paths. Proverbs 3:5-6

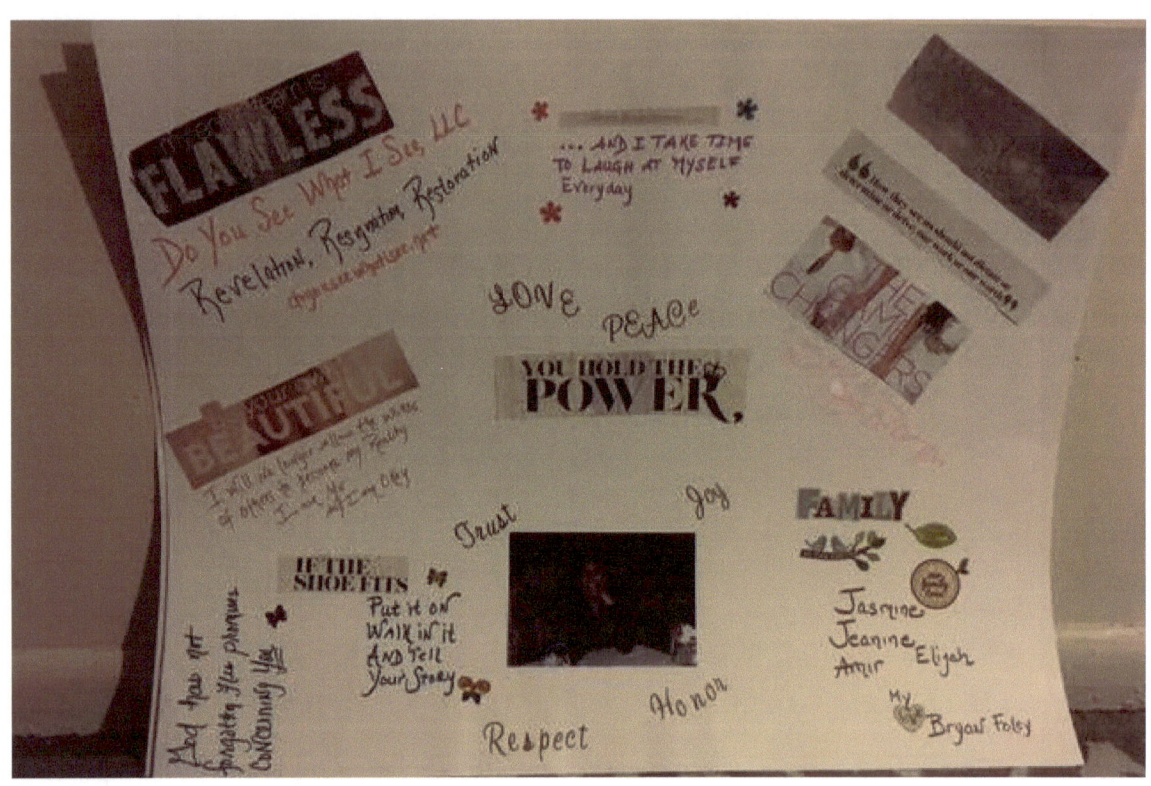

Cherisa Allen

Michelle Dawson

Each element on my Spiritual Vision Board represents my growth as transforming from a caterpillar to a beautiful butterfly. I am finding peace, as I learn to balance life, love my family, encourage friends, and build a safe home and village by taking one-step at a time. I have learned to enjoy music, poetry, and food, to laugh more, find my natural beauty within my radiant brown skin, never giving up hope, being a blossoming entrepreneur, building an inheritance for my children, and serving others while enjoying each glorious day. I am grateful to serve a God who gives me the strength on this Journey to Live the Best Life He has planned for me!!!!

Health & Wellness Spiritual Vision Boards

Doreen Wilder, attended Dr. Cris Spiritual Vision Board Workshop

"When I first created my (spiritual) vision board, it wasn't very difficult because I have always set personal and professional goals. What I had never done before is pray to God specifically for help reaching a goal; I normally would just ask for strength or wisdom to make good decisions that would help me reach my goals. After creating the (spiritual) vision board, I placed it in my bathroom so I could see it before I went to bed each night and as I woke each morning. Now when I pray to God, I ask His hand in guiding me towards meeting each goal and speak to Him about what actions I can specifically take that will help me reach the goals I placed on my board. By praying this way, I have found that I am more focused and have the faith that with God's blessings, he will lead me towards the path that will fulfill my goal or set me in an even better direction. I am happy to let you know that I have made significant progress on each of the 5 goals I have set and am filled with even more faith in God's greatness."

Alicia Domico

Personal, Spiritual, & Professional Growth
Spiritual Vision Boards

"Creating my (spiritual) vision board allowed me a quiet moment to think, center myself, connect with God and open up to the desires already in my heart, some placed there by me and the others by God. Creating my (spiritual) vision board was peaceful; it gave me a sense that my dreams will still come true if I change the way I believe in God and think about myself. Since the creation of my (spiritual) vision board, I've experienced a greater love for myself and goals (I'm not last on my list anymore). I also know that what I believe and say will come to pass.

Professionally - I relaunched my business, Events By Deb, Inc.: We are a full service event & wedding planning company. You may have seen us around town – at Johnson C. Smith, Lake Norman High School, the Black Expo Tour, Brook Valley Community Events or at Weddings in the Charlotte/Triad area!

Personal – The word "no" comes easily without an explanation, and my focus is more centered on God and loving myself first and then others."

Deb Browne
Event Planner, attended Dr. Cris Spiritual Vision Board Workshop

Osceola Thomas,
Author & Entrepreneur,
attended Dr. Cris spiritual vision board workshop

Leticia Parra, Graphic Illustrator, attended Dr. Cris Spiritual Vision Board Workshop

"Using the spiritual vision board process has shifted my paradigm of how to think about prayer and God's principles for creating a visual pictorial of my deepest desires."

"This board has helped me both personally and professionally by keeping me focused on my goals. It helps me with daily, weekly, and monthly planning. It also inspires me to keep going through challenging times."

Takara Edwards, former student of Dr. Cris

"I want to thank Dr. Cris for this "Visual Prayer" experience. Through the process of creating my board, I've had some old dreams and goals rekindled as well as some new dreams and goals that have been ignited. Without this opportunity, these endeavors may have never been realized. Thank you Dr. Cris for allowing the Lord to use you in this powerful way!" D.A. Stewart Style

Desmond Stewart, Entrepreneur

Dr. Cris

"I'm so thankful for God's favor, blessings, mercy and wisdom on how to enhance my prayer experience through using spiritual vision boards."

Dr. Cris

Alicia Domico

Alicia Domico

Faith Based Spiritual Vision Boards

Inspired by Nancy Patton
Created by Desmond Stewart

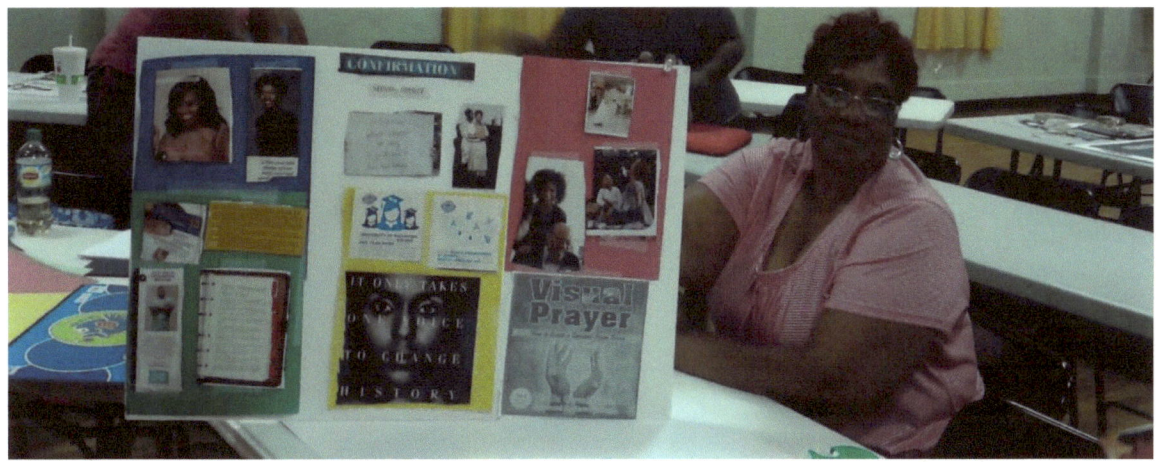

Joan Marshall with her spiritual vision board, attending a workshop at Second Calvary Baptist Church.

Spiritual Vision Boards from Mrs. Bonita Gaither-Davis, Second Calvary Baptist Church member, for Myra Lewis (left) & Sydney Lewis (right).

"The day you taught me how to do a Spiritual Vision Prayer Board was truly a blessing. Thank you Dr. Cris for your guidance. I thank Miss Myra Lewis and Sydney Lewis for the inspiration, and most of all, I give thanks to God for the gift."

More of my students Career Dream Boards

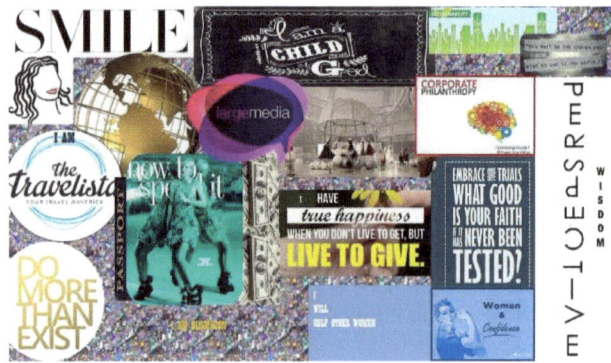

NaShell Simpson

Daryl Dendy

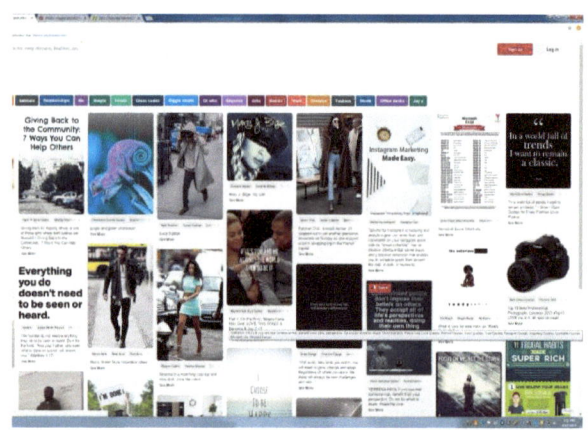

Kiara Gardner
"The dream board helped me develop an actual plan when it comes to my career and future. It also helped me specify and narrow down certain things I want to attain in life."

Gekiia Medley

Frances Rebollo
"With this project I learned what my set goal could be. I mentioned throughout the quarter I had no idea what I was aiming for. The project forced me to really think if I had one choice, what job would I want. I also learned what my mantras are because before I never had one.

Hector Garcia

"It wasn't until I created a (spiritual) vision board that I had validation that everything in God's plan was closely related to the aspiration I visually set forth. Although I went through trials and tribulations regarding work related issues, I had the support of my mentor Dr. Green Brown and a physical (spiritual) vision board that help me align my aspirations and desires into clear manifestations. Now I'm the proud store manager of Aldo Shoes in Northlake Mall, and I'm known as the "business unicorn" of the Charlotte Aldo district, being that I am the younger store manager in the region at 20 years old. Best of all, I eagerly await graduation which is just a few months away with my bachelor's degree in Retail Marketing and Fashion Merchandising."

Lisa Gaitlin

Alicia Nemon
"I learned more about myself through working on the career board. It was helpful to physically see my goals and my values. It's important for people to have a clear idea of what their dream job is so that it will be easier for them to achieve it."

Charity Hines

Astrid Montenegro
"I can now easily go to my board to remind myself of my goals. It is motivating and inspiring. It will also keep me on track."

Postscript

God's Expectation of His Children

As Christians, we are told to live in the world but not of it; this means that we live in a world where immorality runs rampant, and some might view it as normal behavior. But Christ holds us to higher standards and expectations, therefore what we may notice going on around us, we must learn not to allow it to impact our way of thinking or behaving.

When I was first introduced to the concept of creating a spiritual vision board through the movie *The Secret*, I only saw one aspect—biblical principles, primarily *ask, believe, receive*. Mark 11:24 share with us "Therefore I tell you, whatever you ask for in prayer, believe that you have received it, and it will be yours." As I studied the *Bible* more and was interested in developing my own spiritual vision board, I decided to do so based on every biblical principle that I was guided to in the *Bible*. Primarily because my first attempt at creating a vision board instead of a *spiritual* vision board failed miserably. Now when I reflect on that first vision board attempt, I know why it didn't work. God's expectation for me is different than His expectations for those who do not know Him or simply are unaware of the connection between the Bible and vision boards. Therefore, He holds me to a different standard than those who simply do not know.

This different standard sort of reminds me of when my sister and I were little and the different expectations that our parents had for us.

Being the oldest girl, my sister was always expected to do more and take the lead. She taught me how to brush my teeth, tie my shoes, and comb my hair. When it came to household chores, she was responsible for the more serious tasks such as cooking and cleaning, where as I completed the simpler tasks such as doing the dishes and taking out the trash.

God has similar expectations for us. As babes in Christ, those who are establishing a new relationship with Him, He's guiding and leading to continue to grow in Him. Therefore, he does not expect the same behavior that He would expect from those who have known Him for much longer. From those who may have been raised in the church and are more familiar with scripture, that's not to say that He doesn't expect our best and to learn and continue to grow in Him. Most importantly, when it comes to aspects of the bible it's important that we give credit where credit is due and acknowledge the origin of the vision board process.

However, *The Secret*, and a host of other vision board coaches, experts and authors give credit to a new age philosophy or thought process called *the law of attraction*. The law of attraction states that "like attracts like", and whatever we are thinking about or focusing on, we will attract. To maximize results, one should focus on positive thoughts to produce positive energy. As a result, what we have focused on such as our goals, visions and dreams for the future can be transformed into reality; which is actually a great idea, but not an original idea or a new age philosophy, for we know in Proverbs 23:7, we will find, "For as a man thinketh in his heart, so is he." In other words, when we think positive thoughts, we evoke positive energy, and if we think negatively, we can expect negative energy and experiences.

God has also shared with us to make our visions clear and plain (Habakkuk 2:2); to write our visions so that we can physically see them, revisit them and pray over them, which is the vision board process in a nutshell. So when you come right down to it, the basic difference between spiritual vision boards and vision boards is that God and His biblical principles are not acknowledged, credited or appreciated in the vision board process, but spiritual vision boards rely heavily and intimately with the Bible, biblical principles and God's glory and goodness.

Prowls Like a Roaring Lion

Sometimes those who do not support God will attempt to cleverly and cunningly persuade and convince others to do or acknowledge what we may question is right or simply good Christian behavior. Things that we may give pause to and consider that for whatever reason what we are thinking or considering taking part in is simply not of God. Think about that moment when Eve was persuaded by the snake to indulge in something that appeared to be as innocent as taking a bite from an apple. But we know that it wasn't the innocence of the apple that was at fault; it was the act of being intentionally disobedient to God. For we know that "Your enemy the devil prowls around like a roaring lion looking for someone to devour." (1 Peter 5:8). Our job as followers of Christ is to be diligently aware of our enemies' presence, and to resist him standing firm in our faith (1 Peter 5:9). When we know better, we should do better, for in James 4:17 he shares "If anyone, then, knows the good they ought to do and doesn't do it, it is sin for them." Just know that God's expectation for His children is to know, acknowledge and honor Him always.

I urge you my friend to consider your choices. Consider all the blessing that God has for you and desires to give you. Be diligent in your perseverance and not easily persuaded. Pray without ceasing and always, always, always keep God first.

References

Opening
Habakkuk 2:2-3

Forward
Philippians 4:8
Romans 4:9b

Chapter 1
Habakkuk 2:2
Joshua 24:15

Chapter 2
Psalm 6:9
Habakkuk 2:2
Ken Davis, *7 Keys to Successful House Groups*

Chapter 3
Jeremiah 29:11
Acts 10:38
John 10:10
Proverbs 16:1-3
Jeremiah 29:11-13

Chapter 4
Exodus 34:10
Romans 12:2
Matthew 21:22
James 4:2-3
Joyce Meyer, *New Day New You*
Matthew 7:7
Jeremiah 29:13
Habakkuk 2:1-2
Proverbs 3:6 (TLB)
Matthew 6:33 (ASW)
Jeremiah 29:13
Genesis 17:1 AMP
Psalm 37:4
Matthew 19:26
Romans 8:28
Psalm 37:4
2 Corinthians 1:3-5
Isaiah 43:1-3
Hebrews 11:1-6
Isaiah 58:11
Lamentations 3:22-25
1 John 4:16
James 1:2-4
Jeremiah 17:7, 8

Isaiah 40:29, 31

Chapter 5
Deuteronomy 2:7

Chapter 6
Matthew 7:7
Habakkuk 2:2
Psalm 84:11
Philippians 4:13
Matthew 18:20
1 John 4:4
Dr. Wayne Dyer, *Wishes Fulfilled*
2 Corinthians 5:21
Deuteronomy 28:13
Matthew 5:14
Colossians 2:7
Isaiah 53:5
Romans 1:7
Ephesians 2:4
Colossians 3:12
1 Thessalonians 1:4
Colossians 1:11
Isaiah 54:14
2 Samuel 9:3
2 Samuel 22:30
Psalm 18:29

Proverbs 30:1
Acts 26:26
Philippians 4:13
Genesis 7:1
Genesis 18:3
Genesis 20:5
Genesis 24:40
Genesis 28:15
Genesis 30:8
Exodus 3:17
Exodus 28:3
Genesis 2:18
Genesis 3:16
Genesis 6:18
Genesis 24:7
Genesis 12:2
Genesis 16:10
Bruce Wilkinson, *The Prayer of Jabez*
Romans 4:17
Genesis 1:1
Proverbs 18:21
Proverbs 23:7
http://www.empower-yourself-with-color-psychology.com/meaning-of-colors.html
http://www.color-meanings.com
Acts 10:34

Chapter 7

Hebrews 11:1
Hebrews 11:3
Matthew 17:20
Hebrews 11:4
The Secret, (the DVD) regarding actions & attitudes
Psalms 40:1; 42:5 & 11; 43:5; 103:5
The Secret (the DVD) regarding Jack Canfield & *Chicken Soup for the Soul*
Nehemiah 8:12
Deepak Chopra, *The Seven Spiritual Laws of Success*, page 25
Luke 6:38
1 Thessalonians 5:18
Ephesians 5:20
Romans 12:12

Chapter 8
Matthew 7:8
Deuteronomy 11:9-12
1 Samuel 23:4
Mark 5:25-34
John 5:5-8

Chapter 9
Isaiah 43.26
Psalms 107
Jeremiah 29:11-13

Chapter 10

Genesis 1:1
Robert Orben Quote
Habakkuk 2:2
John 1:1-5
Ezra 7:9
Proverbs 3:9-10
1 Corinthians 2:9

Chapter 11

Alicia Domico, Spiritual Vision Board Coach, Ohio

Lisa Alvarez, Life & Spiritual Vision Board Coach, California

Susanne Calman, Spiritual Vision Board Coach, Australia

Cherisa Allen, Spiritual Vision Board Coach, Michigan

About the Author

Dr. Crystal Green Brown is a Spiritual Life Coach, who is certified in and specializes in career development, health/nutrition, and education. As the owner of Ask Dr. Cris, the Spiritual Life Coach & Speaker, LLC (AskDrCris.com,) she empowers clients to live a healthy and well-balanced life by developing customized lifestyle solutions. She has co-authored inspirational books such as *Mosaic Cross, Spirit of the Poet* and *Miracles*. Dr. Green Brown has authored the popular dietary lifestyle book, *How to Be Schoolgirl Skinny,* which was featured in *Diets in Review* and *Today's Charlotte Woman*. This weight loss and health management book is the perfect guide for developing and maintaining a healthy lifestyle. As a College Professor instructing career, marketing, and research courses, this rising Charlottean was honored as a recipient of Who's Who in Black Charlotte Entrepreneurs and dedicates her life to improving the health, wellness, and spirituality of others all over the world.

www.ingramcontent.com/pod-product-compliance
Lightning Source LLC
Chambersburg PA
CBHW041541220426
43664CB00002B/16